Sharing the Knowledge

A First Nations Resource Guide

Researched and compiled by Gene Joseph,
Aboriginal Management Consultants

United Native Nations • Legal Services Society

© 1992, Legal Services Society of B.C.

This material may not be sold for more than the Legal Services Society list price.

Contents may not be commercially reproduced but any other reproduction is encouraged.

The Legal Services Society (LSS) was established in 1979 to make sure that people who cannot afford a lawyer can get one through the legal aid program and to provide education and information about the law to British Columbians.

Development:
    Sadie Kuehn, Schools Program, LSS, and
    Viola Thomas and Theresa Tait, Native Programs, LSS

Prepared for:
    United Native Nations and Legal Services Society

Researched and compiled by:
    Gene Joseph, Aboriginal Management Consultants

Editor:
    Lois Richardson, Publishing Division, LSS

Copy editor:
    Joy Tataryn

Designer:
    Helen Krayenhoff, Publishing Division, LSS

For copies of this publication, please write to:

Distribution Clerk
Legal Services Society
Box 3, Suite 300
1140 West Pender Street
Vancouver, B.C. V6E 4G1

Canadian Cataloguing in Publication Data

Joseph, Gene.
    Sharing the knowledge

    Includes index.
    ISBN 0-919736-77-7

    1. Indians of North America - Canada - Bibliography. 2. Indians of North America - Canada - Government relations - Bibliography. I. United Native Nations. II. Legal Services Society of British Columbia. III. Title.

Z1209.2.C3J67 1992   016.3231'197071   C92-092379-8

Acknowledgements

We would like to thank the following people and organizations for their contributions and assistance in the development of this resource guide. Their support and interest in this project was invaluable.

Theresa Tait, Native Programs, Legal Services Society

Penny Bain, Schools Programs, Legal Services Society

Lionel R. R. Chartrand, Chartrand Law Office, The Pas, Manitoba

En'owkin International School of Writing

Dan George, Prince George Native Friendship Centre

Peter Grant, Hazelton, B.C.

Norma Hall, Nicola Valley Tribal Council

Nancy Hannum, Legal Resource Centre, Legal Services Society

Sharon Jacobs, Council for Yukon Indians

Bill McLennan, University of British Columbia Museum of Anthropology

Maxine Pape, Theytus Books

Millie Poplar, Union of British Columbia Indian Chiefs

Stuart Rush, Rush, Crane, Guenther and Adams

Vicky Russell, Office of the Hereditary Chiefs of the Gitksan and Wet'suwet'en

Don Sawyer, Native Adult Education Resource Centre

Christine Scotnicki, V. Starr & Associates

Vina A. Starr, V. Starr & Associates

Mary Tastad, Native Law Centre, University of Saskatchewan

M. Tenesse, Ktunaxa/Kinbasket Tribal Council

Rosalee Tizya, United Native Nations

Bernie Whiteford, United Native Nations

Photo credits
UBC Museum of Anthropology, *pages 6, 25, 45, 58.*
Alexis MacDonald-Seto, *pages vi, 16, 20, 40, 64, 74.*

Table of contents

Foreword vi

Introduction vii

Part I: History and Culture

General reference 2

Culture 6

Early history 14

Fur trade 17

Church relations 19

Treaties 22

Indian Act 24

Government relations 29

Part II: Current Issues

Social issues 34

Child welfare 37

Education 41

Criminal justice 44

Environmental protection 50

Constitution 53

Aboriginal title — British Columbia 56

Aboriginal title — Canada 61

Aboriginal rights 67

Part III: Future

Self-government 72

Appendices & Indexes

Appendix 1 — Publishers and distributors 80

Appendix 2 — Speakers 87

Subject index 89

Title index 92

Foreword

Sharing the Knowledge: A First Nations Resource Guide was developed with the direct involvement and control of First Nations people. It is hoped that First Nations and their allies will use this resource to understand the legal history of First Nations people and the impact of colonization upon them. It is through greater understanding of our history and a commitment from others to accept aboriginal people as distinct nations that we can co-exist and live in harmony with each other.

This resource guide is a reflection of how we can work together to provide balanced information. It may assist us in reaching greater understanding so that we can work together to end the oppression and racism that continue to prevail in today's society.

Theresa Tait
(Wet'suwet'en Nation)

Director,
Native Programs

Legal Services
Society

Introduction

Canada celebrated the 125th anniversary of Confederation on July 1, 1992. However, for aboriginal peoples, history extends backwards for centuries, and First Nations treaties with European colonial powers predate Confederation. Throughout Canada's history, aboriginal peoples have struggled to have their rights recognized. The resources in this guide document their struggle.

Events such as the blockage of the Meech Lake Accord on the Constitution and the confrontations at Oka and in other areas of Canada have significantly raised awareness of aboriginal issues. While support for aboriginal peoples has increased, there remains a need to educate the public on the issues.

The United Native Nations and the Legal Services Society, Native Programs and School Programs, wish to promote education on aboriginal legal issues. Therefore, this resource guide, which has been produced with assistance from the Law Foundation of B.C., is being made available to schools in British Columbia.

Publications included in the resource guide are written from a First Nations/aboriginal perspective and reflect current First Nations and government positions as well as judicial interpretations. Substantial change in policy and interpretation of the law followed entrenchment of aboriginal rights in the Constitution Act, 1982. Therefore, the emphasis is on material published after 1982.

Only resources that are readily available are included. Although many scholarly theses and academic and technical journals contain excellent articles, they were excluded because they are difficult to find.

The guide is in three parts. Part I contains resources that introduce First Nations culture and history and highlight the historic foundations of aboriginal rights and government relations. Part II presents resources on current issues facing First Nations. Part III presents resources on future directions for achieving recognition of aboriginal rights, specifically entrenchment of the inherent right to self-government in the Constitution or through settlement of aboriginal title.

Within subject areas in each part, citations are listed alphabetically by author. Most citations follow the format: author's name; name of publication; city of publication; name of publisher; date of publication; number of pages; illustrations, photographs, maps, or bibliography, if any.

Readability

Literacy levels are provided to assist teachers in selecting materials at the appropriate reading level. Readability tests serve as a guide to the approximate grade level that must be achieved to read and understand the material. Standard tests use formulas based on word length (number of syllables), sentence length, and number of sentences in a paragraph.

Tests were conducted on the resources by entering and assessing three passages of approximately 100 words each, using Grammatix software. Reading level scores are high because many words common to First Nations are long — tribal names and words such as constitution, self-government, aboriginal.

Therefore, caution is required in using these readability levels since no consideration is given to previous knowledge of the readers. For example, many of the resources include multi-syllable words, such as government and legislation, which are easily understood by grade 12 law students.

In addition, writing style in a publication may be uneven, resulting in different reading grade levels. This is particularly true for groups of articles published in one book.

Although reading levels are not definitive, these three tests are useful in assessing whether materials may be used independently or with teacher support and guidance.

The following tests were used for materials included in this resource guide.

Flesch Reading Ease (FRE)

The formula for the Flesch Reading Ease test is:

- Multiply the average number of words in a sentence by 1.015.
- Multiply the number of syllables per 100 words by .846.
- Add the two results.
- Subtract the total from 206.835.

The higher the score, the easier the reading.

Score	Reading Difficulty	Approximate Grade Level
90 - 100	Very Easy	Grade 5
80 - 90	Easy	Grade 6
70 - 80	Fairly Easy	Grade 7
60 - 70	Standard	Grade 8 - 9
50 - 60	Fairly Difficult	Grade 10 - 12
30 - 50	Difficult	University
0 - 30	Very Difficult	University graduate

FOG Index (FI)

The formula for the FOG Index test is:

- Add the average number of words per sentence to the number of words with three or more syllables.
- Multiply the total by 0.4.

The result is the reading grade level.

Flesch-Kincaid (FK)

The formula for the Flesch-Kincaid test is:

- Multiply the average number of words per sentence by .39.
- Multiply the average number of syllables per word by 11.8.
- Add the two results.
- Subtract 15.59 from the total.

The result is the reading grade level.

Note: The results of each of these tests, done on the same material, vary somewhat. All three scores are provided in citations as well as a general reading grade level based on a combination of the three tests.

When the reading level is given as "College," it indicates a reading level of the first two years of university; when the reading level is given as "University," it indicates a reading level of third-year university and above.

Availability

Publications cited may be purchased through bookstores or directly from the publisher. Addresses of publishers cited are provided in the appendix. Costs are current as of March 1992, but subject to change by publishers.

Federal government reports published by Supply and Services Canada are available from the department listed as the author.

Some publications are out of print and are available only from libraries. These are noted in the citations. Other publications may be available only from third-party distributors — these are also noted. Materials such as videotapes that are available only by rental are also noted.

Publications may also be available at your local resource centre or library or through an inter-library loan.

Part I

History and Culture

General reference

1
British Columbia. Ministry of Native Affairs. **The aboriginal peoples of British Columbia: A profile.** Victoria, B.C.: Ministry of Native Affairs, 1990. [26] p.; illus.

This government document provides a directory of tribal councils in the province. Locations of the tribal councils are identified on maps, and each member band is identified along with its population, economic base, and linguistic affiliation. Very brief descriptions are also given of the history, language, and First Nations' culture.

Reading level: Not applicable (legislative document)
Cost: free

2
British Columbia. Ministry of Native Affairs. **A guide to native organizations and services in British Columbia.** Victoria, B.C.: Ministry of Native Affairs, 1991. 59 p.

This directory of native organizations in the province lists organizations by function (arts and culture, business, education, friendship centres, housing, sports, social services, etc.) as well as bands and tribal councils. Information correct as of March 1991; 1992 edition scheduled.

Reading level: Not applicable (legislative document)
Cost: free

3
Brizinski, Peggy. **Knots in a string: An introduction to native studies in Canada.** Saskatoon: University of Saskatchewan, 1989. 387 p.; illus.; maps; glossary.

Brizinski's extensive compilation of material on the history and cultures of Canada's First Nations should prove useful to scholars and general interest readers. She examines current issues (e.g., native-state relations; aboriginal rights; self-government) within the context of historical events that shape today's reality. She then discusses these issues from the perspective of natives in the North. Coverage of the wide-ranging topics is brief and more descriptive than analytic.

Reading level: College
(FRE = 38   FI = 17   FK = 14)
Cost: $35.50

4
Canada. Indian and Northern Affairs. **Basic departmental data — 1990.** Ottawa: Supply and Services Canada, 1990. 101 p.; tables.

This document provides extensive statistical information on registered Indian populations in Canada. Data for on/off reserve populations include life expectancy, death and mortality rates, infant mortality, tuberculosis, education enrolment, children and adults in care, social assistance, housing, labour force, income, funding arrangements, Indian-administered expenditures, and INAC expenditures. These statistics are updated yearly.

Reading level: College
(FRE = 30   FI = 17   FK = 13)
Cost: free

5
Canada. Indian and Northern Affairs. **The Canadian Indian.** Ottawa: Supply and Services Canada, 1990. 102 p.; illus.

This government document provides a general overview of Canadian Indian cultures, post-contact history, impacts upon the culture, the treaties, the Métis, Indian Act, government policies, land claims, and new developments in self-government and the Indian Act. Generally good, but contains some errors as well as government interpretations.

Reading level: Grade 9
(FRE = 59   FI = 12   FK = 9)
Cost: free

6

Duff, Wilson. **The impact of the white man: The history of Indians of British Columbia.** Victoria, B.C.: Provincial Museum of Natural History and Anthropology, 1965, 1987. 117 p.; illus.

This report, now in its sixth reprint since 1965, remains a standard introductory text for native studies. The impact of the fur trade, missionaries, and colonial Indian policy are highlighted in this three-part text. The section on population change is excellent; however, Duff's discussion of current conditions requires cautious interpretation. Comments reflect viewpoints three decades old.

Reading level: Grade 12
(FRE = 44   FI = 16   FK = 13)
Available from: library loan (out of print)

7

FM Studio for the Children's Project. **Native lands then and now.** North Vancouver: FM Studio for the Children's Project, 1990. Map.

Non-native people used anthropological, historical, and government sources and consulted with tribal councils to compile this map. The map shows comprehensive claim areas, reserve and band locations, linguistics information, glaciation, and possible migration routes. It also has a corner insert of the Lower Mainland area and village/camp sites. The back of the map has a calendar of historic events from the 1700s to 1990 as well as a glossary of terms, statistical information, etc. The information is excellent; however, the size of the print makes it extremely difficult to read.

Reading level: Grade 11
FRE = 52   FI = 15   FK = 11)
Cost: $9.95

8

Frideres, James S. **Native peoples in Canada: Contemporary conflicts.** 3rd ed. Scarborough, ON: Prentice-Hall Canada, 1988. 444 p.; bibliography.

Frideres' third revised edition covers the major post-contact historical events in Indian-white relations in Canada and their impact upon current issues of today's Indian people. He analyzes the Indian Act, treaties, land claims, demographic and social conditions, urbanization, political development, the Métis, and self-government. Good basic reference book.

Reading level: Grade 12
(FRE = 39   FI = 17   FK = 12)
Cost: $20.66

9

Harris, Cole R. **Historical atlas of Canada. Vol. 1, From the beginning to 1800.** Toronto: University of Toronto Press, 1987. illus.; maps; graphs.

This highly recommended publication, which took more than a decade to complete, traces Canadian history from 8000 B.C. to A.D. 1800. Hundreds of Canadian scholars contributed to this publication. Sixty-seven colour plates translate complex events and subject matter into attractive and easily understood visual presentations. Volume 1 is in five parts. Part 1 covers pre-contact history and describes First Nations cultures and population movement (e.g., plates include trade routes and trade articles of B.C. tribes). Also recommended is the section titled "The Northwest," which traces expansion of the fur trade. Another section illustrates settlement of the eastern Atlantic and St. Lawrence River regions. Primary and secondary references are provided for each of the 67 plates for further research.

Reading level: Grade 11
(FRE = 49   FI = 14   FK = 11)
Cost: $90

10

Logie, Patricia Richardson. **Chronicles of pride: A journey of discovery.** Calgary: Detselig Enterprises, 1990. 196 p.

This publication presents portraits of 31 Canadian aboriginal leaders, many of whom are from B.C. These individuals, from a variety of backgrounds and occupations, provide strong role models in their efforts to improve lives of aboriginal people.

Short biographical sketches and the artist's impressions of their personalities bring the portraits to life. A positive book. Teacher's guide is available.

Reading level: Grade 10
(FRE = 62   FI = 13   FK = 10)
Cost: $27.95; $17.95 for teacher's guide

11

Marsh, James H., ed. **The Canadian encyclopedia.** 2nd ed. Edmonton: Hurtig, 1988. 4 vols.

The Canadian Encyclopedia was updated and expanded into four volumes in this second edition. Approximately 10,000 entries by specialists in their respective fields cover all aspects of Canadian history and culture. Information on aboriginal peoples may be found under tribal name, or by subject area. Subjects covered include treaties, aboriginal rights, Royal Proclamation of 1763, land claims, native religion, native social conditions. Information provided is concise and objective, reflecting great care in research and editing. While oversights are inevitable in such a massive undertaking, on the whole, the encyclopedia deserves its reputation as an outstanding Canadian reference work.

Reading level: College
(FRE = 33   FI = 18   FK = 13)
Cost: $100 for 4 volumes

12

Mintz, Helen, Theresa Goode, and others. **Multicultural week, February 19-25, 1989: Aboriginal cultural diversity; A resource package for secondary schools.** Vancouver: B.C. Teachers' Federation, 1989. 63 p.; bibliography.

This booklet contains lesson ideas on B.C. First Nations. Sections of interest on legal issues include "To potlatch or not to potlatch"; "Native land claims"; and "Indian reserve simulation." The simulation game introduces students to the social, economic, and political issues involved in living on reserve.

Reading level: Grade 11
(FRE = 57   FI = 14   FK = 11)
Cost: $4

13

Morrison, Bruce R., and Roderick C. Wilson, eds. **Native peoples: The Canadian experience.** Toronto: McClelland and Stewart, 1986. 542 p.; photos; maps.

Numerous authors contributed to this dry, fact-filled book. Though Morrison and Wilson question the appropriateness of an anthropological perspective, they proceed to present it on wide-ranging topics that are organized according to geo-cultural subdivisions. Historical information on each cultural group contains extensive information on life-style, beliefs, and values.

Reading level: Grade 12
(FRE = 42   FI = 16   FK = 13)
Cost: $29.95

14

National Film Board of Canada. **Our home and native land: A film and video resource guide for aboriginal Canadians.** 3rd ed. Winnipeg: National Film Board of Canada, 1991. 44 p.

This guide lists over 100 films and videos produced and distributed by the National Film Board of Canada. The eight subject areas include "Foundations of nationhood"; "Our nation's wealth"; "Skills not lost"; "In company with nature"; "Aboriginal rights and land claims"; and "Native women's issues." Information includes a short description of the item, year of production, running time, order number, and price.

Reading level: College
(FRE = 40   FI = 19   FK = 15)
Cost: free

15

Reiter, Robert A. **The fundamental principles of Indian law.** Edmonton: First Nations Resource Council, 1990.

This reference guide on native law is intended for use by lawyers and advisers of First Nations government. Information is provided on relevant legislation, regulations, implementation, and administration. The guide includes chapters on band councils' powers and procedures under the Indian Act; conducting business on reserves; tax laws; labour law; and wills and estates. The publication, in loose-leaf format, is to be updated with bulletins from the publisher four times a year. A table of cases and an index are provided. (The annotated edition did not include GST in taxation issues, nor did it include the *Sparrow* decision in the section on fiduciary duty.)

Reading level: College
(FRE = 26   FI = 19   FK = 15)
Cost: $105

16

Sawyer, Don, and Art Napolean. **Effective instruction of native adults: 1 - 6.** Salmon Arm, B.C.: Native Adult Education Resource Centre, 1991. 6 VHS videocassettes; 15 minutes each; colour.

This video series presents native and non-native adult educators discussing concerns relevant to native adult education. Each video concentrates on a particular issue: community-based adult education, student-centred learning, building culture into the curriculum, native learning/teaching styles, life skills, and counselling. Produced by/for First Nations people.
Recommended and annotated by Don Sawyer, Native Adult Education Resource Centre.

Cost: $10

17

Sawyer, Don. **Native English curriculum guidelines: A handbook for adult education.** Salmon Arm, B.C.: Native Adult Education Resource Centre, May 1991. [300] p.

Besides general perspectives on teaching English to native adults, this resource also includes theme units on Indian self-government, community development, land claims. It provides experiential exercises. This book was originally prepared for the Native Education Centre in Vancouver and was produced by/for First Nations people.
Recommended and annotated by Don Sawyer, Native Adult Education Resource Centre.

Reading level: College (provided by annotator)
Cost: $15.60

18

Vancouver Public Library. History and Government Division. **Native land claims in Canada: A study guide.** Vancouver: Vancouver Public Library, October 1990. 21 p.

This guide was developed for doing research in the Vancouver Public Library. However, it will prove useful to other libraries and researchers of native Indian people's history, culture, and issues. Short annotations are provided for periodicals and indexes, bibliographies, basic reference works, and maps and atlases. It also has a short list of some of the major native organizations.

Reading level: Grade 11
(FRE = 39   FI = 15   FK = 11)
Cost: free

19

Woodward, Jack. **Native law.** Toronto: Carswell, 1989, 1990. 626 p. (loose-leaf).

This handbook of native law is intended for practitioners and advisers, but should also be of value to general researchers. Subject headings include bands, membership, government under the Indian Act, land management and development, taxation, and family law. Each subject includes an examination of key legal issues, applicable law, and areas of possible contention. The text includes tables of authorities, provincial and federal statutes, and cases.

Reading level: College
(FRE = 29   FI = 19   FK = 16)
Cost: $115 (loose-leaf); $55 (hardbound)

Culture

20
Atleo, E. Richard. "Policy development for museums: A First Nations perspective." **B.C. Studies** 89 (Spring 1991): 48-61.

Atleo applies an abstract theory from his doctoral dissertation to provide some explanation for repatriation of museums to First Nations. He considers resolution of this issue to be essential to righting some of the injustices done to First Nations and proposes guidelines for museum policies that are based on mutual respect.

Reading level: College
(FRE = 67   FI = 21   FK = 16)
Cost: $10

21
Cole, Douglas, and Ira Chaikin. **An iron hand upon the people: The law against the potlatch on the Northwest Coast.** Vancouver: Douglas & McIntyre, 1990. 230 p.; illus.

The potlatch is a central legal, political, and social institution among the Indian people of British Columbia. The government sought to suppress it between 1884 and 1951. This well-researched book covers government methods to enforce the law, its impact upon the Indian people, and their response to this law. Primary focus is on the Kwakiutl and the Gitksan, although other First Nations of B.C. are mentioned.

Reading level: Grade 12
(FRE = 44   FI = 16   FK = 13)
Cost: $29.95

22
George, Leonard. "Native spirituality, past, present, and future." **B.C. Studies** 89 (Spring 1991): 160-168.

This article provides some insights into the contrasts between the value systems of natives and non-natives. George focuses on the Wheel of Life to discuss some of the spiritual aspects of native philosophy. He then offers personal interpretations of this philosophy, which may assist both individuals and societies in improving their lives.

Reading level: Grade 8
(FRE = 65   FI = 12   FK = 8)
Cost: $10

Chief's whaler hat
Nuu-chah-nulth
made by Mrs. Jessie Webster

photo: J. Gijssen

23

Kelly, Patrick. "The value of First Nations languages." **B.C. Studies** 89 (Spring 1991): 141-148.

In a world where change is the norm, language as a vehicle for cultural expression remains essential to preserving First Nations heritage and identity. Kelly quotes recommendations from recognized native and non-native authorities to support this argument. He further suggests both natives and non-natives will benefit from any initiatives to preserve First Nations languages.

Reading level: Grade 12
(FRE = 30   FI = 18   FK = 13)
Cost: $10

24

McMillan, Alan D. **Native peoples and cultures of Canada: An anthropological overview.** Vancouver: Douglas & McIntyre, 1988. 307 p.; photographs; maps.

McMillan's overview of native Canadian life is subdivided according to geo-cultural areas. He acknowledges that the broad scope in both time and geography limits coverage of each of the 12 topic areas. An important shortcoming is a lack of information on the role of women in native society. He only briefly discusses the socialization of children and youth. The narrative style makes this book highly readable.

Reading level: Grade 12
(FRE = 41   FI = 16   FK = 12)
Cost: $19.95

25

Suttles, Wayne, ed. **Handbook of North American Indians: Northwest Coast, Vol. 7.** Washington, D.C.: Smithsonian Institution, 1990. 777 p.; illus.; bibliography.

Suttles provides good ethnographic and post-contact historical descriptions of the native peoples of the Northwest Coast, including Tlingit, Haida, Tsimshian (Nisga'a, Gitksan, and Coast Tsimshian), Haisla, Bella, Oowekeeno, Bella Coola, Kwakiutl, Nuu-chah-nulth, Northern Coast Salish (Comox, Pentlatch, and Sechelt), and the Central Coast Salish (Squamish, Halkomelem, Nooksack, Northern Straits, and Clallam). This basic reference book has an excellent bibliography; however, it is not organized by subject.

Reading level: College
(FRE = 42   FI = 17   FK = 13)
Cost: $38 (U.S.)

26

Union of B.C. Indian Chiefs. **Potlatch: A strict law bids us dance.** Vancouver: Union of B.C. Indian Chiefs, 1975. 16 mm film or 1/2" videocassette: 53 minutes (film); 23 minutes (edited videocassette); colour; sound.

An exemplary film that portrays the potlatch and the government's attempts to abolish the potlatch. It should be used in conjunction with the book *Potlatch or Persecution*.

Available from: Legal Services Society
Rental: free

Culture — Beaver

27

Brody, Hugh. **Maps and dreams: Indians and the British Columbia frontier.** Vancouver: Douglas & McIntyre, 1981. 297 p.; illus.; maps; bibliography.

This land use and occupancy study is based on 18 months of fieldwork among the Beaver people of northeastern B.C. Odd-numbered chapters discuss events in the community from a personal perspective while even-numbered chapters present Beaver culture and history in an academic fashion. The result is an outstanding work that portrays the Beaver people's attachment to their land and the effects of industrialization on their life-style. Maps illustrate hunting, trapping, and food gathering areas of First Nations in the northeast part of the province.

Reading level: Grade 12
(FRE = 48   FI = 12   FK = 12)
Cost: $14.95

28

Napolean, Art. **Native studies of North Eastern B.C.** Salmon Arm, B.C.: Native Adult Education Resource Centre, 1991. 179 p.

Written by a Cree educator from the area, this volume presents information on native history in northeastern B.C. It is divided into three sections: early Indian people, contact and colonization, and the recent decades. Interviews with elders and secondary materials were used in compiling this guide. Activities and perspectives applicable to all native groups are included. Produced by/for First Nations people. *Recommended and annotated by Don Sawyer, Native Adult Education Resource Centre.*

Reading level: Grades 8-10 (provided by annotator)
Cost: $15

29

Ridington, Robin. **Trail to heaven: Knowledge and narrative in a northern native community.** Vancouver: Douglas & McIntyre, 1988. 291 p.

This unique compilation of legends and conversations explores and contrasts the thought, world, and knowledge sources of the B.C. Beaver people with Western culture. Ridington's narrative incorporates both introspection and retrospection as he attempts to reach some understanding of the "real people's" philosophy and values. An excellent, highly readable look at the rich, diverse life and thoughts of the Dunne-za.

Reading level: Grade 8
(FRE = 71   FI = 11   FK = 8)
Cost: $14.95 (paperback); $29.95 (hardbound)

Culture — Carrier

30

Moran, Bridget. **Stoney Creek woman: The story of Mary John.** Vancouver: Tillacum Library, 1988. 142 p.; photographs.

This compelling narrative engages the reader in the joys and pain of Mary John's life, a life shadowed by the hardships endured by her people — racism, sickness, and poverty. We see her personal struggle to rise above these indignities as a child in residential school and as an independent Carrier woman. Both moving and thought-provoking, this is a story of Mary's journey of hope and of personal and cultural survival.

Reading level: Grade 7
(FRE = 77   FI = 9   FK = 7)
Cost: $9.95

31

Thorner, Thomas, ed. **SA TS'E: Historical perspectives on northern British Columbia.** Prince George, B.C.: College of New Caledonia Press, 1989. 570 p.

This compilation of 29 short essays is intended for a history course. It provides a current review of major aspects of the history of northern B.C. Several essays relate to the missionaries and Carrier, Sekani, Beaver, and Nishga [sic] people. Included is a description of the life of Kwah, a Carrier chief; Treaty 8; and a former Lejac student's life in the residential school. Though generally well referenced, the book makes many assumptions to fill information gaps. Easy to read and informative.

Reading level: College
(FRE = 42   FI = 16   FK = 13)
Cost: $39.90

Culture — Coast Salish

32

Duff, Wilson. **The Upper Stalo Indians of the Fraser Valley, British Columbia.** Victoria, B.C.: British Columbia Provincial Museum, Department of Education, 1952. 136 p.; illus.; maps; bibliography.

This report, based on fieldwork carried out in 1950, describes traditional Upper Stalo community life and the use of natural resources. A discussion of relations with neighbouring villages is included with three maps depicting Stalo territory.

Reading level: Grade 10
(FRE = 62   FI = 12   FK = 10)
Available from: library loan (out of print)

33
Suttles, Wayne. **Katzie ethnographic notes.** Edited by Wilson Duff. Victoria, B.C.: British Columbia Provincial Museum, 1955, 1986. 92 p.; maps; bibliography.

This report, based on fieldwork carried out in Katzie in 1952, provides an overview of Katzie territory, place names, and traditional use of resources. Includes maps of Katzie territory, as identified to Suttles by the natives.

Reading level: Grade 12
(FRE = 61   FI = 14   FK = 12)
Cost: $6.75

34
Suttles, Wayne. **Coast Salish essays.** Vancouver: Talonbooks, 1987. 340 p.; illus.; maps; bibliography.

A collection of 16 essays by a leading ethnographer provides a new look at Coast Salish culture. Of particular interest are the Part 1 discussion of traditional Salish culture and the Part 3 review of adaptation and survival following colonization. Suttles challenges older anthropological theories and hypotheses about the Coast Salish. Using thorough research skills, he presents papers with new viewpoints on cultural adaptations to the environment, spiritual beliefs, the meaning of community, and language.

Reading level: College
(FRE = 26   FI = 20   FK = 16)
Cost: $19.95 (paperback); $29.95 (hardbound)

35
Wells, Oliver N. **The Chilliwacks and their neighbors.** Vancouver: Talonbooks, 1987. 228 p.; photographs; maps.

This compilation of Oliver Wells' lifelong work demonstrates his involvement in preserving and re-establishing the cultural traditions of the Chilliwack people. The chronological transcript excerpts provide insight into the process he used to acquire information and knowledge from elders. Awkward phrasing, repetition, and constant clarification of Halkomelam words makes reading difficult, but it is interesting.

Reading level: Grade 6
(FRE = 84   FI = 9   FK = 6)
Cost: $18.95

Culture — Gitksan/Wet'suwet'en

36
Delgamuukw et al v. the Queen: Proceedings at trial. Vancouver: United Reporting Service, 1990. 369 vols.

Volumes 1 to 143, 153 to 161 contain evidence by Gitksan and Wet'suwet'en people regarding their history and culture. While the transcripts are lengthy and rather difficult to read, they contain valuable firsthand information on all aspects of their culture and history without secondary interpretation. Volumes 162 to 369 contain "expert" (anthropologists, historians, etc.) interpretations and observations on the Gitksan and Wet'suwet'en peoples' history, culture, and lands.

Reading level: Grade 6
(FRE = 82   FI = 9   FK = 6)
Available from: The Office of Hereditary Chiefs, Hazelton, B.C., or the Office of Hereditary Chiefs, Vancouver, B.C., for in-house use (by appointment only).

37
Cassidy, Maureen. **Proud past: A history of the Wet'suwet'en of Moricetown, B.C.** Moricetown: Moricetown Band, 1980. 48 p.; illus.; bibliography.

The history of Moricetown begins with a legend on the origin of the tribe. In chapter 1, a short description of culture is given (unfortunately oversimplified), followed by the impact of the fur trade and missionaries. The three remaining chapters document changes and difficulties arising from being forced off traditional lands by settlers and the government. The history concludes on the optimistic note that the young people are learning traditional ways.

Reading level: Grade 7
(FRE = 70   FI = 9   FK = 7)
Cost: $4

Culture — Haida

38

Blackman, Margaret B. **During my time: Florence Edenshaw Davidson, a Haida woman.** Vancouver: Douglas & McIntyre, 1982. 172 p.; illus.

This is a biography of a remarkable Haida woman born in 1896. She reveals, with gentle strength and dignity, the roles and work of Haida women and their family life. She also discusses the adaptations of the Haida people to Christianity, Western civilization, and government practices, while maintaining traditional Haida culture. Recommended for its portrayal of Haida life today.

Reading level: College
(FRE = 53   FI = 17   FK = 14)
Cost: $14.95

39

MacDonald, George F. **Chiefs of the sea and sky: Haida heritage sites of the Queen Charlotte Islands.** Vancouver: University of British Columbia Press, 1989. 95 p.; illus.; maps; bibliography.

MacDonald provides a description of eighteen Haida villages, four of which are located in South Morseby National Park. He bases his work on archival photographs and records from 1880 to 1910. In Part 1, an overview of traditional Haida culture is presented, thus giving an appreciation of the people who created the imposing buildings and sculptures depicted in the following two sections.

Reading level: Grade 12
(FRE = 47   FI = 15   FK = 12)
Cost: $15.95

Culture — Kwakiutl

40

Assu, Harry, and Joy Inglis. **Assu of Cape Mudge: Recollections of a coastal Indian chief.** Vancouver: University of British Columbia Press, 1989. 163 p.; illus.; maps; bibliography.

This autobiography of a Kwakiutl Cape Mudge chief born in 1905 recounts the origins of his people according to oral history. More current topics include the political organization of the band; the village's development in the areas of education, religion, and recreation; their relationship to and the use of ocean resources; the chief's experience as a commercial fisher; the potlatch; and the return to Cape Mudge of confiscated art from the Canadian government. This is not an anthropological text but a readable account of an Indian person's life as he lived it.

Reading level: Grade 9
(FRE = 67   FI = 12   FK = 9)
Cost: $19.95 (paperback); $29.95 (hardbound)

41

Jonaitis, Aldona, ed. **Chiefly feasts: The enduring Kwakiutl potlatch.** Vancouver: Douglas & McIntyre, 1991. 300 p.; illus.; bibliography.

Although this book was created as a catalogue, its photographs and five essays illustrate the cultural role and importance of the potlatch to the Kwakiutl. Essays on government attempts to stop the potlatch and the Kwakiutl response to the potlatch law are nicely completed with a description of a modern potlatch. Kwakiutl contributions to this book ensure this part of their culture is properly represented and portrayed.

Reading level: Grade 12
(FRE = 52   FI = 14   FK = 12)
Cost: $45

42

Chuck Olin Associates and U'mista Cultural Centre. **Box of treasures.** Watertown, MA: Documentary Educational Resources, 1983. VHS videocassette; 28 minutes; colour.

This video presents the Kwakiutl of Alert Bay, as they redefine their cultural identity while constructing a centre to house masks and other potlatch valuables. The documentary also considers the changing role of language, art, and cultural events in the present society.

Available from: U'Mista Cultural Centre
Cost: $35

Culture — Nuu-chah-nulth

43

Kirk, Ruth. **Wisdom of the elders: Native traditions on the Northwest Coast. The Nuu-chah-nulth, Southern Kwakiutl and Nuxalk.** Vancouver: Douglas & McIntyre, in association with the British Columbia Provincial Museum, 1986. 256 p.; photographs; illus.; map; bibliography.

The Nuu-chah-nulth, Southern Kwakiutl, and Nuxalk people are highlighted in this publication, which is intended to replace the outdated *Our Native People* series. The emphasis is on the similar environment shared by the three tribes. "The world that was" chapter presents traditional culture and society. "Time's flow" highlights the impact of white people on the tribes. Continuity of traditions is shown through the combination of oral history of tribal elders and contemporary photographs of cultural events with historical and ethnographic accounts and archival photos. Care has been taken to present First Nations' viewpoints, and the large number of illustrations reinforce the text. This is a good introductory publication, but combining in one volume three distinctive groups, each with its own history and institutions, tends to result in generalizations that may confuse readers.

Reading level: Grade 9
(FRE = 65   FI = 12   FK = 9)
Cost: $24.95

44

Efrat, Barabara S., and W.J. Langlois. **Nu-tka: The history and survival of Nootkan culture.** Victoria, B.C.: Ministry of the Provincial Secretary and Travel Industry, [1978]. 65 p.; illus.; photographs; bibliography.

This book is described as a 5,000-year perspective of west coast history. Part 1 describes traditional Nuu-chah-nulth culture and use of resources. Here, archaeological information dates First Nations' occupation of the area to 2300 B.C. Part 2 describes some aspects of contemporary Nuu-chah-nulth culture. These descriptions are based on aural history recordings of various Nuu-chah-nulth people by the B.C. Provincial Archives. Of particular interest are the descriptions of preparations for a potlatch.

Reading level: Grade 8
(FRE = 64   FI = 11   FK = 8)
Available from: Crown Publications

45

Jones, Chief Charles, with Stephen Bosustow. **Queesto: Pacheenaht chief by birthright.** Nanaimo, B.C.: Theytus Books, 1981. 125 p.; photographs.

At 100 years of age, Chief Jones relates his life story. He begins life in a longhouse and as a child learns fishing and food-gathering skills from his father and family. He provides an ongoing comparison of beliefs and values as he speaks of first contact with white people, missionaries, and reserves. He shows us a life in transition while offering hope for a future with a strong people and culture. Good reading.

Reading level: Grade 8
(FRE = 82   FI = 10   FK = 8)
Cost: $14.95

46

St. Claire, Denis, Louis Clamhouse, Joshua Arima, E.Y. Edgar, Charles Jones, and John Thomas. **Between Ports Alberni and Renfrew: Notes on West Coast peoples.** Mercury Series paper 121. Ottawa: Canadian Museum of Civilization, 1991. 323 p.

Nuu-chah-nulth elders from the west coast of Vancouver Island provide the authors with oral history reviews as part of their strategy to preserve the Nuu-chah-nulth history. This report presents oral history, place names, and maps. Use of symbols in Indian names and words may create some reading difficulty.

Reading level: Grade 12
(FRE = 39   FI = 17   FK = 13)
Cost: $19.95

Culture — Okanagan

47

Carstens, Peter. **The Queen's people: A study of hegemony, coercion, and accommodation among the Okanagan of Canada.** Toronto: University of Toronto Press, 1991. 333 p.; photographs; maps; bibliography.

In this sociological study of a reserve community, Carstens examines relations within the community, with the surrounding non-native community, and with government. As background to the study, Part 1 presents an overview of Okanagan culture and history during the fur trade and gold rush and the period involving missionaries. The introduction of the Indian Act and reserve allotments are also covered. Part 2 examines socio-economic development, local government, and political factionalism in the community during the past four decades.

Reading level: University
(FRE = 24   FI = 23   FK = 18)
Cost: $23.95

48

Hill-Tout, Charles. **The Salish people: The local contribution of Charles Hill-Tout. Vol. 1: The Thompson and the Okanagan.** Edited by Ralph Maud. Vancouver: Talonbooks, 1978. 176 p. illus.; maps.

This is one of four volumes containing the reports and field notes of Hill-Tout, a self-taught ethnographer who conducted research among Salish peoples from 1895 to 1911. Part 1 provides a brief overview of Nlaka'pamux culture, and includes ten myths. Part 2 on the Okanagan includes a list of place names and myths.

Reading level: Grade 12
(FRE = 48   FI = 17   FK = 13)
Cost: $14.95

Culture — Sechelt

49

Peterson, Lester. **The story of the Sechelt nation.** Sechelt, B.C.: Sechelt Indian Band, 1990. 145 p.

Over a 30-year period the author visited the Sechelt people, learning their history, language, and spiritual beliefs. His writings are now published by the Sechelt Indian Band. His work provides interesting comparisons to mythological, religious, and historical events worldwide. Contains many Sechelt words.

Reading level: Grade 9
(FRE = 63   FI = 12   FK = 9)
Cost: $15.95

Culture — Secwepemc (Shuswap)

50

Caffey, John, Ed Golstgrom, and others. **Shuswap history: The first 100 years of contact.** Kamloops: Secwepemc Cultural Education Society, 1990. 59 p.; photographs; illus.; maps; bibliography.

This historical account of the 17 Secwepemc (Shuswap) bands begins with Alexander Mackenzie's travels through their territories in 1793. The book highlights the impact on the natives of the fur trade, the gold rush, the epidemics of the 1850s and 1860s, and missionary activities. The struggle for land during the allotment of reserves concludes this publication. Includes archival photographs and maps of Secwepemc territory.

Reading level: Grade 7
(FRE = 67   FI = 10   FK = 7)
Cost: $13.95

Culture — Sliammon

51

Kennedy, Dorothy, and Randy Bouchard. **Sliammon life, Sliammon lands.** Vancouver: Talonbooks, 1983. 176 p.; photographs; illus.; maps; bibliography.

These authors present a cultural and historical description of the Sliammon, Homalco, and Klahoose people. These descriptions are based primarily on oral history gathered from elders during 1977 and 1981. Numerous photographs illustrate daily life and food gathering practices. Historical information is highlighted in chapters 11 to 13 and covers the period from early exploration to missionary activities and establishment of reserves.

Reading level: Grade 9
(FRE = 65   FI = 11   FK = 9)
Cost: $16.95

Culture — Tsimshian

52

Seguin, Margaret, ed. **The Tsimshian: Images of the past, views for the present.** Vancouver: University of British Columbia Press, 1984. 343 p.; illus.; map.

This is a collection of 13 academic papers presented at a 1979 conference in Hartley Bay. The papers cover a wide variety of subjects including archaeology, mythology, and material culture of the Tsimshian. Most of the articles are more suited to anthropologists than the general public. Two exceptions are "Hartley Bay: A History," by Ken Campbell, and "Images of the Nineteenth Century Economy of the Tsimshian," by James MacDonald. These two articles discuss Tsimshian participation in the economy during the 1800s.

Reading level: College
(FRE = 45   FI = 17   FK = 14)
Cost: $37.95

Culture — Taku Tlingit

53

Emmons, George Thornton. **The Tlingit Indians.** Vancouver: Douglas & McIntyre, 1991. 488 p.; illus.; bibliography.

This major ethnographic work is based on the observations of George T. Emmons while he resided among the Tlingit during the 1880s and 1890s. It is historically valuable in that the information has never been published before. Recommended as a basic reference work on the Tlingit.

Reading level: College
(FRE = 53   FI = 17   FK = 14)
Cost: $75

Early history

54

Adams, Howard. **Prison of grass: Canada from a native point of view.** Saskatoon: Fifth House, 1989. 208 p.; bibliography.

A classic account of Canadian history from a native perspective. The author draws on both history and personal experiences to illustrate racism toward native people. The fur trade, western expansion, and the Northwest Rebellion of 1885 are examined in depth using native sources, which contradict official versions. Originally published in 1975, this has been updated with statistical data from the 1986 census.

Reading level: Grade 11
(FRE = 51   FI = 14   FK = 11)
Cost: $18.95

55

Batllori, S.J., Miguel. "The papal division of the world and its consequences." In **First images of America: The impact of the new world on the old,** Vol. 1, edited by Fredi Chiappelli, 211-220. Berkeley: University of California Press, 1976.

Batllori examines a longstanding problem in interpreting the significance of the papal bulls which divide the New World between the Spanish and Portuguese. He thinks the Alexandrine Bulls only authenticate existing treaties between the two kingdoms and do not confer legitimate title of the Americas to the Spanish. Rather, the bulls relate primarily to concessions of privilege concerning the evangelization of the Indian people.

Reading level: College
(FRE = 37   FI = 22   FK = 16)
Available from: library loan (out of print)

56

Davies, Maureen. "Aspects of aboriginal rights in international law." In **Aboriginal peoples and the law: Indian, Métis and Inuit rights in Canada,** edited by Bradford Morse, 16-46. Ottawa: Carleton University Press, 1989.

This article considers the historical basis for aboriginal rights in international law. The topic is introduced with a discussion of papal bulls and writings on aboriginal rights by the 16th-century Spanish philosopher Viitoria. The status (sovereignty) and territorial rights of aboriginal people under international law are then examined. The author finds that concepts have been inappropriately applied by domestic courts to justify seizure of land. Failures also arise from lack of knowledge of aboriginal culture and institutions.

Reading level: College
(FRE = 28   FI = 18   FK = 15)
Cost: $31.95

57

Green, L. C., and Olive P. Dickason. **The law of nations and the new world.** Edmonton: University of Alberta Press, 1989. 303 p.; bibliography.

These authors examine the legal, theological, and philosophical doctrines that rationalize expansion and colonization. In Part 1 Green analyzes international law at the time of discovery with reference to medieval European laws and customs, the letters of commissions granted to explorers, papal bulls, and scholarly writings. In Part 2, "Concepts of sovereignty at the time of first contact," Dickason considers theological and philosophical arguments to justify colonization and subjugation of natives of the Americas. The author further examines views of theologians opposed to this treatment of the natives. The writings of the 16th-century Dominican missionary Las Casas exemplify the opposition.

Reading level: University
(FRE = 31   FI = 22   FK = 19)
Cost: $30

58

Johnston, Darlene. **The taking of Indian lands in Canada: Consent or coercion?** Saskatoon: University of Saskatchewan Native Law Centre, 1989. 93 p.

Historically, there is a perception that transfer of First Nations' land to government took place in an "orderly and principled" fashion. This study questions the accuracy of this assumption, beginning with the Royal Proclamation of 1763 when British government directed that land not be taken from tribes against their will. Colonial governments' adherence to the proclamation is examined with reference to historic documents. Policies and legislation implemented after Confederation are then reviewed, including treaties and Indian Affairs administration.

Reading level: College
(FRE = 34   FI = 18   FK = 14)
Cost: $12

59

Koning, Hans. **Columbus: His enterprise.** New York: Monthly Review Press, 1991. 141 p.

Popular history places Columbus in the role of hero for his "discovery" of the Americas. This book presents Columbus in a more realistic light. In 1492, Christopher Columbus sailed from Spain searching for Asia. Through miscalculation, the three ships became lost, landed on the island of Dominica, and initiated the genocide and slavery of native peoples of the islands.

Reading level: Grade 10
(FRE = 61   FI = 13   FK = 10)
Cost: $6

60

Miller, J. R. **Skyscrapers hide the heavens: A history of Indian-white relations in Canada.** Toronto: University of Toronto Press, 1989, 1991. 351 p.; illus.; maps; bibliography.

This study of Indian-white relations in Canada spans five centuries. Part 1 chronicles the period prior to 1800 when the French, English, and First Nations were partners in trading and military alliances. Part 2, aptly titled "Coercion," discusses westward expansion and governments' efforts to assimilate and "civilize" First Nations by making treaties and creating reserves. A discussion of native peoples' reaction includes the Northwest Rebellion. Relations in the 1900s are covered in Part 3, which closes with political action surrounding the 1982 repatriation of the Constitution. (The author's opinion on this issue differs from that of First Nations.) A 1991 reprint of the book includes a chapter on confrontations at Oka, rejection of the Meech Lake Accord, and occupation of INAC offices.

Reading level: Grade 12
(FRE = 42   FI = 16   FK = 12)
Cost: $35

61

O'Malley, John W. "The discovery of America and reform thought at the papal court in the early Cinquecento." In **First images of America: The impact of the new world on the old,** Vol. 1, edited by Fredi Chiappelli, 185-200. Berkeley: University of California Press, 1976.

This extensively referenced chapter examines Rome's general policy of reform, which explains its political agenda affecting the New World. The reform goals include securing world peace and expanding Christian territories to achieve Christian universality. The philosophy that God "wills all men to be saved" animates much of the reform thought and directs conversion tactics among the aboriginal peoples of America.

Reading level: College
(FRE = 34   FI = 20   FK = 16)
Available from: library loan (out of print)

62

Trigger, Bruce. **Natives and newcomers: Canada's heroic age reconsidered.** Kingston: McGill-Queen's University Press, 1986. 430 p.; illus.; bibliography.

Past accounts of the history of New France characterize early settlers and missionaries as heroically struggling against a hostile environment while Indian people are depicted as savages. Trigger disputes this version of history using archaeological, anthropological, and historical documents to reinterpret early Canadian history.

Reading level: University
(FRE = 27   FI = 21   FK = 18)
Cost: $19.95

63

Weckmann-Munoz, Luis. "The Alexandrine Bulls of 1493: Pseudo-Asiatic Documents." In **First Images of America: The impact of the new world on the old,** Vol. 1, edited by Fredi Chiappelli, 201-207. Berkeley: University of California Press, 1976.

This author uses extensive references to support his claim that Pope Alexander VI acted on historically recognized authority when he drew the north-south "Alexandrine Line" to settle a land dispute between the Spanish and Portuguese. The 1493 bull, written by Columbus, grants the "islands" — including America — he found to the Spanish crown on condition that the natives be converted to Christianity.

Reading level: University
(FRE = 21   FI = 25   FK = 21)
Available from: library loan (out of print)

Blanket
Chilkat

photo: Alexis MacDonald-Seto

Fur trade

64

Brown, Jennifer S. H. **Strangers in blood: Fur trade company families in Indian country.** Vancouver: University of British Columbia Press, 1980. 255 p.; illus.; bibliography.

Brown uses biographical records, including letters, journals, wills, and court records, to analyze social relations in the fur trade era. Unions between native women and fur traders during the period prior to 1821 are examined in depth, as are relations between the parents, their children, and their employers. The author finds that permanency and status of the unions were influenced by the philosophy of the Hudson's Bay Company and the North West Company as well as regulations governing employee conduct. This book provides a personal perspective on Indian, Métis, and white relations during this period.

Reading level: College
(FRE = 31   FI = 20   FK = 17)
Cost: $16

65

Fisher, Robin. "Indian control of the Maritime fur trade and the Northwest Coast." In **Sweet promises: A reader on Indian-white relations in Canada**, edited by J. R. Miller, 279-293. Toronto: University of Toronto Press, 1991.

This short article opposes popular opinion that Indian people were naive traders. Instead, the author reveals that Indians of the Northwest Coast were accomplished traders who often refused to trade for goods they did not need. In addition, the Indian people maintained their internal controls over trade routes. Traditional government systems are revealed when ship captains note that chiefs were primary contacts in negotiations.

Reading level: Grade 11
(FRE = 51   FI = 15   FK = 11)
Cost: $24.95

66

Fisher, Robin. **Contact and conflict: Indian-European relations in British Columbia, 1774-1890.** 2nd ed. Vancouver: University of British Columbia Press, 1992. 280 p.; bibliography.

This extensively researched work by Fisher has become a classic in the study of Indian-white relations. The sea and land-based fur trade is portrayed as a mutually beneficial relationship that did not substantially alter aboriginal culture. The decline of the fur trade and the colonial administration under Governor Douglas is discussed. The different attitudes of fur traders and settlers toward native people are outlined, followed by discussion of the activities of miners and missionaries and the demands of settlers that led to efforts to eliminate native culture and traditional use of territories.

Reading level: Grade 12
(FRE = 47   FI = 15   FK = 12)
Cost: $21.95

67

Krech III, Shepard, ed. **The subarctic fur trade: Native social and economic adaptations**. Vancouver: University of British Columbia Press, 1984. 183 p.

Seven papers by different authors challenge existing beliefs about native economic history and social adaptations in the context of the fur trade. Various theories are proposed to explain the development of — or limits in — native dependency, all relating to changes in traditional life-style and depletion of resources. The complex, scholarly arguments are not always clear. Case studies include the James Bay and Moose Factory Cree.

Reading level: College
(FRE = 44   FI = 18   FK = 15)
Cost: $19.95

68

Newman, Peter C. **Caesars of the wilderness: Company of adventurers**. Vol. 2. Markham, ON: Viking Penguin Inc., 1987. 434 p.; bibliography.

This "unauthorized" history documents events from the founding of the North West Company in 1783 to the surrender of the Hudson's Bay Company's monopoly in 1869. During this period, economic rivalry develops slowly but finally erupts in violence and becomes a struggle for power and territory. Here, historical figures gain a new dimension as Newman recreates the life and times of the voyageur and fur trader.

Reading level: College
(FRE = 43   FI = 18   FK = 15)
Cost: $6.95 (paperback); 29.95 (hardbound)

69

Ray, Arthur J. "Periodic shortages, native welfare, and the Hudson's Bay Company 1670-1930." In **The subarctic fur trade: Native social and economic adaptations**, edited by Shepard Krech III, 1-20. Vancouver: University of British Columbia Press, 1984.

Ray challenges the commonly held belief that modern native welfare societies are recent, post-World War II phenomena resulting from government involvement. He asserts native welfare was imbedded in fur trade activities where Indian people were considered "assets" to the Hudson's Bay Company.

Reading level: College
(FRE = 29   FI = 20   FK = 16)
Cost: $19.95

70

Ray, Arthur J., and Donald B. Freeman. **Give us good measure: An economic analysis of relations between the Indians and the Hudson's Bay Company before 1763**. Toronto: University of Toronto Press, 1978. 298 p.; illus.; maps; bibliography.

These authors examine the fur trade from an economic perspective. They introduce the subject with an overview of fur trade history and European and Indian cultures at the time of contact. The structure of the Hudson's Bay Company is then examined and trade relations discussed. Ceremonial gift-giving prior to trading is described and expenses analyzed. The authors use Hudson's Bay account records to compile extensive statistical data as part of their analysis of the economics of trading relations. Of particular interest are the tables on trade equivalents and "overpluses." These are the excess amounts or surpluses obtained by increasing the terms of trade over official prices.

Reading level: Grade 11
(FRE = 54   FI = 14   FK = 11)
Available from: library loan (out of print)

71

The other side of the ledger: An Indian view of the Hudson's Bay Company. Ottawa: National Film Board of Canada, 1972. Film or VHS videocassette; 42 minutes; colour; sound.

Indian people reveal the Hudson's Bay Company's stranglehold on the economy and lives of northern and western Canada's Indian people. Exploitive policies and actions of the Bay are still remembered and have relevance today, despite some outdated statistical information.

Cost: $26.95
Rental: $5/week

72

Van Kirk, Sylvia. **Many tender ties: Women in fur-trade society in western Canada, 1670-1870.** Winnipeg: Watson & Dwyer, 1980, 1986. 303 p.; illus.; maps; bibliography.

In many native tribes, marriage has traditionally been a means of strengthening ties between communities. Women served as envoys while contributing equally to the family's livelihood. In this book, the union of native women and fur traders is examined, using extensive research from HBC and North West Company post journals and diaries. Native women are shown to have been instrumental in improving and expanding trade relations. The clash of cultures, the reaction of colonial society to the unions, and the racism encountered by children of the "country marriages" illustrate effectively race relations at the time.

Reading level: Grade 12
(FRE = 45   FI = 17   FK = 13)
Cost: $12.00 (paperback); $24.95 (hardbound)

Church relations

73

Graham, Elizabeth. **Medicine man to missionary: Missionaries as agents of change among the Indians of southern Ontario, 1784-1867.** Toronto: Peter Martin Associates, 1975. 121 p.; maps; bibliography.

Graham's study of the roles and goals of missionaries (to save and civilize) relies on historical missionary documents. These missionaries act on or resist prevailing government policy and effect social, cultural, and economic changes among the Indian people. This ethnocentric description contains few references to Indian people's response to change.

Reading level: College
(FRE = 44   FI = 19   FK = 16)
Available from: library loan (out of print)

74

Grant, John Webster. **Moon of wintertime: Missionaries and the Indians of Canada in encounter since 1534.** Toronto: University of Toronto Press, 1984. 301 p.

This extensive analysis traces the encounters of Indian people with Christianity over 450 years. Grant examines both the aims and activities of missionaries of all denominations and the varying responses of Indian people at different times and under different circumstances. He neither justifies nor condemns. He argues that Indian people's embracing of Christianity filled a void in their spiritual life which was a consequence of contact between differing cultures.

Reading level: College
(FRE = 35   FI = 18   FK = 15)
Cost: $17.95

75

Lillard, Charles, ed. **Mission to Nootka, 1874-1900: Reminiscences of the west coast of Vancouver Island.** Sidney, B.C.: Gray's Publishing, 1977. 119 p.; photographs; bibliography.

Excerpts from Father Brabant's journal chronicle his life among the Nootka where he "singlehandedly" creates order by changing a civilization. Throughout, he pursues his goal of Christianizing and "civilizing." He provides important accounts of ceremonies and rituals of the Nootkan people. However, his generalizations about the Nootkans and their culture are offensive: they typify beliefs and language use of the time.

Reading level: Grade 11
(FRE = 63   FI = 15   FK = 11)
Available from: library loan (out of print)

76

Lillard, Charles, ed. **Warriors of the North Pacific: Missionary accounts of the Northwest Coast, the Skeena and Stikine Rivers, and the Klondike, 1829-1900.** Victoria, B.C.: Sono Nis Press, 1984. 247 p.; bibliography.

Lillard compiles and annotates excerpts from four historical works to make them accessible to a wider reading audience. His intent is to fill a "gap" in Northwest Coast history by relating it from the perspective of missionaries who lived and worked with Indian people. These four eye-witness accounts provide superficial though useful descriptions of Indian culture and the transitional period.

Reading level: College
(FRE = 45   FI = 20   FK = 16)
Cost: $16.95

77

Mullhall, David. **Will to power: The missionary career of Father Morice.** Vancouver: University of British Columbia Press, 1986. 221 p.; photographs; bibliography.

Morice dreams of becoming a missionary priest-king and becomes one in Carrier territory. His successful quest for power is explained in terms of his personality, the supportive frontier environment, and his use of the "Durieu system." Oral histories provide insight into the Indian people's response to the man and to Christianity. This biography presents an informative account of Indian-white relations during the early 1900s.

Reading level: Grade 12
(FRE = 44   FI = 16   FK = 12)
Cost: $29.95

78

Nock, David A. **A Victorian missionary and Canadian Indian policy: Cultural synthesis vs cultural replacement.** Waterloo, ON: Wilfrid Laurier University Press, 1988. 160 p.; bibliography.

An analysis of Wilson's life with the Indian people in Ontario (1868-1893) provides a case study of the different policies and programs affecting Indian culture. Initially, Wilson singlemindedly pursues cultural replacement via residential schools. By 1891, he begins to covertly advocate cultural synthesis — a process that recognizes the Indian people's independence and autonomy. He retires in discouragement, seeing little hope for such drastic change in his time.

Reading level: Grade 12
(FRE = 50   FI = 15   FK = 12)
Cost: $14.95

79

Patterson II, E. Palmer. **Mission on the Nass: The evangelization of the Nishga (1860-1990).** Waterloo, ON: Eulachon Press, 1982. 147 p.; bibliography.

Christianity spreads among the Nishga [sic] beginning with their invitation to an Anglican mission in 1864. Patterson examines missionary-Nishga relations and describes missionary attitudes, actions, and responses to the Nishga people. Material drawn from missionary accounts provides a brief but biased view of Nishga culture.

Reading level: College
(FRE = 28   FI = 18   FK = 15)
Available from: library loan (out of print)

Dorothy Grant

photo: Alexis MacDonald-Seto

80

The Devil and Mr. Duncan. Victoria, B.C.: Sono Nis Press, 1985. 335 p.; photographs; bibliography.

Murray attempts to balance historical depictions of this Anglican missionary as either a monster or a saint. After first encounter in the 1850s, Duncan acts to "save" some demoralized Tsimshians from the "rapacious white society" by relocating them to Metlakatla, an isolated new settlement. Despite hardships and fierce opposition, he persists in his belief that it was necessary to soften the blow of cultural shock and to advance the cause of aboriginal rights — an intriguing view.

Reading level: Grade 9
(FRE = 63   FI = 12   FK = 9)
Cost: $16.95

81

Usher, Jean. **William Duncan of Metlakatla: A victorian missionary in British Columbia.** Ottawa: National Museum of Canada, 1974. 134 p.; bibliography.

Written in newspaper form, this case study considers Metlakatla to be a social experiment for change that failed. Extensive analysis of Duncan's social and theological beliefs as well as missionary ideology give some explanations for formation of the "Christian industrial utopia." Lasting 15 years, the experiment succeeds in some areas but ultimately fails, because Duncan does not fully appreciate the role of traditional leaders in Tsimshian society. Non-biographical.

Reading level: College
(FRE = 42   FI = 18   FK = 15)
Cost: $3.95

82

Whitehead, Margaret. **Now you are my brother: Missionaries in British Columbia.** Sound Heritage Series No. 34. Victoria, B.C.: Provincial Archives of British Columbia, 1981. 92 p.; photographs.

Reminiscences from a variety of sources portray missionary influence on the lives of Indian people from the 1870s to the 1950s. This descriptive, non-judgmental review consists of interview transcripts from white (mostly) and Indian people. Though missionaries did succeed in nominally Christianizing most of the province and in effecting some cultural changes, we see examples of Indian people's resistance and selectivity.

Reading level: Grade 8
(FRE = 64   FI = 11   FK = 8)
Cost: $5.65

83

Whitehead, Margaret. **The Cariboo mission: A history of the Oblates.** Victoria, B.C.: Sono Nis Press, 1981. 135 p.; photographs.

This story objectively traces the Catholic priests' presence among and relationships with Chilcotin, Shuswap, and Carrier people between 1866 and 1960. The Oblates' task was to "civilize and save" Indian people. Despite ongoing resistance, they worked toward their goal by applying the "Durieu system" for conversion by educating the children. Extensive use of names and place names is confusing but effective.

Reading level: Grade 12
(FRE = 46   FI = 17   FK = 13)
Cost: $9.95

84

Whitehead, Margaret, ed. **They call me father: Memoirs of Father Nicolas Coccola.** Vancouver: University of British Columbia, 1988. 192 p.; bibliography.

A lengthy introduction, packed with historical events and their interpretations, provides some insights into Indian-white relations in B.C. during the 1800s. Coccola presents himself as an ordinary missionary who zealously applies Bishop Durieu's harsh and culturally destructive system to "save" the Indian people. Coccola's edited memoirs chronicle his advancement through B.C. villages where he touches and changes the lives of many.

Reading level: Grade 10
(FRE = 65   FI = 12   FK = 10)
Cost: $15.95 (paperback); $29.95 (hardbound)

Treaties

85

Bartlett, Richard H. **Indian reserves and aboriginal lands in Canada; A homeland; A study in law and history.** Saskatoon: Native Law Centre, University of Saskatchewan, 1990. 218 p.

Historically, lands set aside for First Nations were intended as homelands. This report addresses the question "Do these lands provide a homeland and basis for independent development?" In answering this question, Bartlett examines laws about ownership, power, and responsibilities concerning reserve lands and land set aside by treaty or agreement. Part 1 considers the history of how lands were set apart. Part 2 discusses the differences between reserve, treaty, and lands set apart by agreement. Part 3 examines federal and provincial roles, and Part 4 considers fiduciary responsibility based on the Guerin decision. The author concludes that government control of Indian land is excessive and suggests that laws applying to Indian lands should be interpreted to enable the lands to be homelands in reality. Tables of cases and authorities are provided.

Reading level: College
(FRE = 38   FI = 18   FK = 14)
Cost: $60

86

Getty, Ian A.L., and Donald B. Smith, eds. **One century later: Western Canadian reserve Indians since Treaty 7.** Vancouver: University of British Columbia Press, 1978. 138 p.; photographs; bibliography.

These conference proceedings focus on historical and contemporary issues relating to southern Alberta's 1877 Treaty 7. Topics include the fur trade, and social, economic, and political developments. We see few successes and many failures as the history of the treaty is traced. In looking to the future, Indian speakers caution against trusting too much — this being one factor that partly explains notable failures.

Reading level: College
(FRE = 32   FI = 20   FK = 16)
Available from: library loan (out of print)

87

Kuhlen, Daniel J. **A layperson's guide to treaty rights in Canada.** Edited by Anne Skarsgard. Saskatoon: Native Law Centre University of Saskatchewan, 1985. 59 p.

This guide provides an overview and discussion of major Canadian treaties and their terms. The paper concludes with a review of court decisions on the effect of entrenchment of aboriginal rights in the Constitution Act, 1982. (Additional details are provided in the three appendices and relate to pre-Confederation treaties, Vancouver Island treaties, and post-Confederation treaties.)

Reading level: College
(FRE = 41   FI = 18   FK = 14)
Cost: $15

88

Madill, Dennis. **British Columbia Indian treaties in historical perspective.** Ottawa: Research Branch, Indian and Northern Affairs Canada, 1981. 112 p.; maps; bibliography.

This is one of the few books providing detailed information on the Vancouver Island treaties signed between 1850 and 1854 and a treaty involving the Coast Salish Indian peoples near Victoria, Nanaimo, and Fort Rupert. Madill also presents Treaty 8, signed in 1899, in which "a small portion of British Columbia [approximately 269 350 km^2 in the northeastern corner of the mainland] was included." Contains relevant treaty copies.

Reading level: College
(FRE = 35   FI = 18   FK = 14)
Available from: library loan (out of print)

89

Marshall, Donald, Sr., Alexander Dermy, and Putus Simon Marshall. "The covenant chain." In **Drumbeat: Anger and renewal in Indian country**, edited by Boyce Richardson, 71-104. Toronto: Summerhill Press, 1989.

The 1752 treaty between the British crown and the Mi'kmaq affirmed Mi'kmaq sovereignty and their right to use and enjoy traditional lands. In this chapter, the Grand Chief of the Mi'kmaq recounts their history up to the time of Confederation. Subsequent government attempts to invalidate traditional Mi'kmaq government and culture are highlighted. Two recent court cases illustrate the provincial and federal governments' failure to honour the treaty of 1752, even though a 1985 Supreme Court decision upheld the treaty. This article effectively demonstrates the source and justification for First Nations' anger and sense of betrayal.

Reading level: Grade 12
(FRE = 45   FI = 14   FK = 12)
Cost: $14.95

90

Mitchell, Michael. "An unbroken assertion of sovereignty." In **Drumbeat: Anger and renewal in Indian country**, edited by Boyce Richardson, 105-136. Toronto: Summerhill Press, 1989.

Mohawk sovereignty was recognized in a treaty over 200 years prior to Confederation. The Grand Chief of the Mohawk explains the Two Row Wampum treaty and the 1795 Jay Treaty, which affirmed Mohawk independence and the right to maintain their laws and customs. He describes resistance to government intrusions and the Mohawk people's struggle to have the treaties recognized. Police raids on Mohawk communities are viewed as examples of the need for a renewal of traditional government as opposed to that created under the Indian Act.

Reading level: College
(FRE = 39   FI = 18   FK = 15)
Cost: $14.95

91

Price, Richard, ed. **The spirit of the Alberta Indian treaties**. 2nd ed. Edmonton: University of Alberta Press, 1987. 202 p.; photographs.

Price reports on the research of the Treaty and Aboriginal Rights Research Group of the Indian Association of Alberta. The differing interpretations by government and First Nations with regard to Treaties 6, 7, and 8 are examined. Negotiations as reported in government documents are recounted, and First Nations' interpretation of the scope and intent of the treaties are presented using interviews with elders.

Reading level: Grade 12
(FRE = 49   FI = 15   FK = 12)
Cost: $14.95

92

Price, Richard. **Legacy Indian treaty relationships**. Edmonton: Plains Publishing, 1991. 156 p.; illus.; photographs.

Highly recommended. This book examines the historical and current relationship between government and First Nations. Section 1 examines why and how treaties were negotiated and the results of the agreements. Section 2 considers the contemporary situation and includes government policy, the Constitution, and topics of negotiations (e.g., one unit is titled "Why is Indian control of Indian education important?"). The six chapters of the text are presented in units. Each unit begins with a focus question, e.g., "How did the Constitution Act of 1982 affect aboriginal and treaty rights?" Background on the issue contains the perspectives of both the First Nations member and government. Discussion questions and topics for further research are provided at the end of each unit as well as definitions of key words introduced in the unit. Illustrations, photographs, and copies of relevant historical documents are used throughout the lessons.

Reading level: Grade 11
(FRE = 42   FI = 15   FK = 11)
Cost: $26.95 (10% discount to schools and libraries)

Indian Act

93

Bartlett, Richard H. **Indians and taxation in Canada.** 2nd ed. Saskatoon: University of Saskatchewan Native Law Centre, 1987. 88 p.

Bartlett examines taxation and tax exemptions of Indian people. A short overview of historic legislation and government policy on taxation of registered and treaty Indians introduces the subject. Then, authority to tax is considered and court decisions on taxation examined. Income tax rulings (both personal and corporate) are closely scrutinized to clarify tax-exempt and non-exempt earnings. Sales tax legislation and administration receive similar treatment. Other taxation, including personal property, succession, and customs, are briefly reviewed. (Note: taxation of lessees of reserve land is altered under the 1988 amendments to the Indian Act.)

Reading level: College
(FRE = 31   FI = 19   FK = 15)
Cost: $25

94

Bartlett, Richard H. **The Indian Act of Canada.** 2nd ed. Saskatoon: University of Saskatchewan Native Law Centre, 1988. 43 p.

Bartlett asserts that the Indian Act has not taken into consideration treaty rights and does not allow self-government. Part 1 considers the history of the Indian Act along with the 1982 entrenchment of aboriginal rights. Then, the membership provisions of the act and the revisions made under Bill C-31 are examined. In Part 3, self-government under the act is reviewed, and Section 88 of the act allowing provincial legislation to apply to First Nations is considered in detail. Inclusion or omissions in the act of provisions agreed to under treaty are examined.

Reading level: College
(FRE = 38   FI = 19   FK = 14)
Cost: $10

95

Canada. Indian and Northern Affairs. **Proposed amendments to the Indian Act concerning conditionally surrendered land and band taxation powers.** Ottawa: Indian and Northern Affairs Canada, 1987.

This government document provides details on background, rationale, and implications of proposed amendments to the Indian Act. The amendments stem from problems identified by the Kamloops Band and include lack of council control of commercial land development on reserve and the inability to tax lessees.

Reading level: Grade 12
(FRE = 44   FI = 16   FK = 12)
Cost: free

96

Canada. Indian and Northern Affairs. **Land, revenues and trusts review: Phase I report.** Ottawa: Supply and Services Canada, 1988. 19 p.

The Auditor General's 1986 report was extremely critical of government management of Indian assets. This prompted the government to conduct a three-phase study to recommend changes to the Indian Act, government regulations, and administration procedures. Phase I identifies seven problem areas that require revision: land management, land registry, trust funds, estates, by-laws, elections, and membership. The report provides background on the current situation in each area, highlights problems and issues of concern, and identifies key issues to be examined in Phase II.

Reading level: College
(FRE = 39   FI = 18   FK = 14)
Cost: free

97

Canada. Indian and Northern Affairs. **Impacts of the 1985 amendments to the Indian Act (Bill C-31): Summary report.** Ottawa: Supply and Services Canada, 1990. 62 p.

In 1990, a joint consultation committee made up of native groups and INAC carried out research to examine the impact of Bill C-31. This report summarizes findings of the four-part study, which included an aboriginal inquiry; a survey of registrants; band and community studies; and review of government programs. The study finds that key areas affected by Bill C-31 are housing, health, and post-secondary education. The report includes financial and statistical data.

Reading level: College
(FRE = 38   FI = 18   FK = 15)
Cost: free

98

Canada. Indian and Northern Affairs. **Indian band membership: An information booklet concerning new Indian band membership laws and the preparation of Indian band membership codes.** Ottawa: Supply and Services Canada, 1986. 26 p.; English/French.

In 1985, Bill C-31 amended the Indian Act. This amendment enables people to regain status, including Indian women and their children. Most women previously lost their status by marrying non-Indians and enfranchised Indians. This booklet explains who can regain their status as well as the amendment's effect upon band membership laws.

Reading level: University
(FRE = 31   FI = 22   FK = 18)
Cost: free

99

Canada. Indian and Northern Affairs. **Land, revenues and trusts review: Phase II report.** Ottawa: Supply and Services Canada, 1990. 142 p.

The Phase II report of the lands, revenues, and trusts review summarizes findings of consultations with First Nations and also includes background technical reports. Phase II presents an overview of land management, land registry, trust funds, estates, by-laws, elections, and membership. Options for change at the legislative and policy level are identified. Discussion then focuses on the impact of the proposals and identifies specific research to be carried out in Phase III of the study. Although technical in nature, the report demonstrates the complexities of changing the Indian Act.

Reading level: College
(FRE = 33   FI = 18   FK = 14)
Cost: free

Eagle frontlet
Kwakwaka wakw from Hope Island

photo: J. Gijssen

100

Hawley, Donna Lea, ed. **The annotated 1990 Indian Act: Including related treaties, statutes and regulations.** 3rd ed. Toronto: Carswell, 1990. 210 p.

This expanded edition provides text of current legislation, notes on court cases, and information on regulations that band government must conform to. Part 1 addresses fishing and hunting rights under treaties. This is followed by information on the Jay Treaty. Part 3 includes sections of the Royal Proclamation of 1763 which deal with aboriginal affairs as well as the Constitution Act, 1867. The 123 sections of the act are considered by subject. The new chapter on band government includes regulations on elections, council procedures, referendums, and borrowing. Of special interest is the Sechelt Indian Band Government Constitution. A chapter is also provided on health and estates.

Reading level: Not applicable (legislative format)
Cost: $36.50 (paperback); $49 (hardbound)

101

Joseph, Shirley. "Assimilation tools: then and now." **B.C. Studies** 89 (Spring 1991): 65-79.

Findings from a national inquiry into the effects of Bill C-31 bring to light numerous problems stemming from a bill intended to end discrimination against Indian women in Canada. Joseph argues that this bill advances government's longstanding intent to assimilate Indian people and concludes that government legislation and policies have been and remain contrary to basic rights and freedoms.

Reading level: College
(FRE = 39   FI = 19   FK = 14)
Cost: $10

102

Kydd, Donna L. **Labour law on reserve.** Vancouver: Native Programs, Legal Services Society, 1992. 42 p.

This is one of a series of booklets by Donna Kydd. This publication contains very basic information on the federal and provincial labour laws applicable on reserves.

Reading level: Grade 10
(FRE = 59   FI = 14   FK = 10)
Cost: free

103

Kydd, Donna L. **Indian land holdings on reserve.** Vancouver: Native Programs, Legal Services Society, 1989. 32 p.

Kydd provides basic readable layperson's information on the Indian Act. The booklet is intended for use by Indian band members who wish to know more about obtaining land on reserve and about the Indian Act land-holding system.

Reading level: Grade 9
(FRE = 60   FI = 13   FK = 9)
Cost: free

104

Kydd, Donna L. **Debtor-creditor law on reserve.** Vancouver: Native Programs, Legal Services Society, 1988. 29 p.

Over half of this booklet covers general debtor-creditor information with additional information on debtor-creditor areas covered by the Indian Act. Good basic information on how the Indian Act may protect property on reserve. However, the act also punishes, since these same laws make credit application more difficult for Indian people than for the general population.

Reading level: Grade 7
(FRE = 71   FI = 11   FK = 7)
Cost: free

105

Reiter, Robert A. **An examination of the evolving concept of band councils, their authorities and responsibilities, and their statutory instruments of power.** Edmonton: First Nations Resource Council, 1990.

Reiter provides a reference guide on band government under the Indian Act. The author presents a framework for an analysis of the legal status, function, liabilities, and statutory powers of band councils. Legal aspects of band by-laws are addressed in detail with references to case law. Individual chapters cover land use and zoning; taxation; and law and order by-laws. The author argues that changes should be made to the Indian Act to clarify legal authority and liability of band councils, and, more importantly, to allow First Nations governments greater autonomy. (The author's example of combining traditional government and elected band councils by using by-law power to delegate authority from band council to traditional bodies will not necessarily reflect self-government views of B.C. First Nations.)

Reading level: College
(FRE = 27   FI = 20   FK = 16)
Available from: library loan (out of print)

106

Sandy, Nancy. **The Indian Act and what it means.** Vancouver: Union of B.C. Indian Chiefs, 1988. 137 p.

A section-by-section interpretation of the Indian Act by a native Indian lawyer for use by laypeople. Subjects covered in the act are: registration and membership, reserve lands, sale or barter of produce, roads and bridges, expropriation of reserve lands, special reserves, surrenders of reserves, and wills.

Reading level: Not applicable (legislative format)
Cost: $14.95

107

Sewid-Smith, Daisy. **Prosecution or persecution.** Alert Bay, B.C.: Nu-Yum-Balees Society, 1979. 97 p.; illus.

In 1884, Canada passed a law forbidding the potlatch. From 1913 to 1932, Indian agent William Halliday enforced this law on the Kwakiutl, imprisoning those who held potlatches and confiscating valuable cultural property. Reports and letters of the Indian agent are reprinted with the memoirs of the people who suffered this oppression.

Reading level: Grade 11
(FRE = 61   FI = 13   FK = 11)
Available from: library loan (out of print)

108

Somewhere between. Vancouver: Hy Perspectives Media Group, 1982. 1/2" Beta or VHS videocassette or 16 mm film; 56 minutes; colour and black and white; sound.

This video sensitively explores the consequences of loss of legal status as an Indian person. Women reveal the effect the loss had on their lives and families, their alienation from their people, and the anguish and anger it brought them. Recommended for use in the study of Bill C-31 materials.

Available from: Legal Resource Centre, Legal Services Society
Rental: free

109

Starr, Vina A. **Pros and cons of doing business on a reserve.** Vancouver: V. Starr & Associates, November 1988. [68 p.] (Unpublished)

This paper presents an overview of taxation issues for Indian businesses on reserve. Recent cases on Indian tax law are discussed. The different ways business can be carried on are explained, along with their tax consequences. Recent amendments to the Indian Act in the taxation area are also explained. Produced for First Nations people. The law presented is as of November, 1988. Prepared for a seminar sponsored by the Centre for Native Small Business. *Recommended and annotated by V. Starr & Associates.*

Reading level: Grade 10 (provided by annotator)
Available from: Legal Resource Centre, Legal Services Society
Cost: photocopying cost

110

Starr, Vina A., and Michael Bush. "Indian self-government and the Indian Act." **Legal Perspectives** 14, no. 4 (May 1990): 16-21.

This journal article summarizes the history of the Indian Act and how it hampers Indian self-government. Produced for First Nations peoples. *Recommended and annotated by V. Starr & Associates.*

Reading level: Grade 10 (provided by annotator)
Available from: Legal Services Society
Cost: free

111

Tobias, John L. "Protection, civilization, assimilation: An outline history of Canada's Indian policy." In **Sweet promises: A reader on Indian-white relations in Canada**, edited by J.R. Miller, 127-144. Toronto: University of Toronto Press, 1991.

This short article outlines the three main thrusts of the Indian Act from pre-Confederation to the present. The first Indian Acts were a direct result of the Royal Proclamation of 1763, in which only the crown could make treaties with Indian nations. This protection of Indian lands changed as a result of Protestant movements to Christianize and civilize Indian people. Assimilation policies followed. Finally, in 1969, the government's White Paper attempted to complete the assimilation policies by repealing the Indian Act. As a result of Indian protest, the White Paper was withdrawn, but "this official withdrawal does not mean that the goal has been repudiated …."

Reading level: University
(FRE = 20   FI = 23   FK = 19)
Cost: $24.95

112

Weaver, Sally M. **Making Canadian Indian policy: The hidden agenda 1968-1970**. Toronto: University of Toronto Press, 1981. 204 p.; bibliography.

Weaver draws on a variety of government information sources as she explores the policy-making process that culminated in the White Paper of 1969. Multiple factors affected the process, including the liberal-democratic Canadian values that sought to eliminate special status for Indian people. Exclusion of the Indian people's viewpoint resulted in a policy that was unanimously rejected. The ethnocentric policy was withdrawn and became an embarrassment to the government.

Reading level: College
(FRE = 32   FI = 19   FK = 16)
Cost: $13.95

Government relations

113
Kahnewake. Ottawa: National Film Board of Canada, 1990. Film or videocassette; 110 minutes; colour; sound.

During the Oka crisis, the Mohawk Indians of Kahnewake supported the Oka Mohawks by blockading the Mercier bridge. This film presents the Mohawk perspective of living in a state of siege under the Quebec provincial police and the Canadian armed forces. (Note: the National Film Board plans to release a film on the Oka crisis.)

Cost: $34.95;
Rental: $5/week

114
Incident at Restigouche. Ottawa: National Film Board of Canada, 1984. Film or videocassette; 46 minutes; colour; sound.

Salmon fishing is an important part of the Micmac Indian people's life in Restigouche, Quebec. In 1981, the Quebec police raided the reserve and charged several Indian people with poaching. This film reveals that the judicial system lacked neutrality and the police were excessively violent and racist. It also demonstrates the Quebec government's role in suppressing Micmac sovereignty and self-government.

Cost: $26.95

115
Canada. Indian and Northern Affairs. **Outstanding business: A native claims policy; Specific claims.** Ottawa: Indian and Northern Affairs Canada, 1982. 33 p.

Specific claims refer to specific actions and omissions of governments relating to obligations under treaty or under legislation such as the Indian Act. (A large number of claims deal with land and management of assets.) This booklet explains government policy on specific claims. Included are short explanations of (1) how government obligations arise under the Indian Act and under treaty and (2) the events leading up to the current policy. Guidelines outline the basis for allowable claims and the government process for assessing and arriving at compensation for successful claims. Note: quarterly reports on current activities may be obtained from the Office of Specific Claims.

Reading level: College
(FRE = 38   FI = 18   FK = 15)
Cost: free

Basket – cedar root, cherry bark, bullrush
Chilcotin

photo: J. Gijssen

116

Davis, Maureen. "Aboriginal rights in international law: Human rights." In **Aboriginal peoples and the law: Indian, Métis and Inuit rights in Canada,** edited by Bradford Morse, 745. Ottawa: Carleton University Press, 1989.

As a member of the United Nations General Assembly, Canada is party to a number of international agreements and accords that protect and promote human rights. This article examines cultural and political rights of indigenous people. Particular reference is made to Sandra Lovelace's appeal to the International Human Rights Committee on the basis of discrimination under section 12-1-B of the Indian Act. The author finds promise in asserting aboriginal rights on an international level. However, she also points out a weakness in the system that results from a lack of enforcement mechanisms.

Reading level: College
(FRE = 28   FI = 18   FK = 15)
Cost: $31.95

117

Hughes, Ken, **Summer of 1990: Fifth report of the standing committee on aboriginal affairs**. Ottawa: House of Commons, 1991.

Military intervention in the Mohawk land claims dispute at Oka was viewed with great concern not only because it involved military action against people of Canada but also because it heralded the possibility of growing militancy among First Nations. This military action resulted from government inaction in addressing the Mohawk land issue. In this report, the Standing Committee reviews events leading up to the raid on Kanesetake. The review is based on testimony of Mohawk people; other First Nations; federal and municipal governments; church groups; and other interest groups. (A list of witnesses heard and location of their evidence in the minutes of the committee is provided in Appendix A.) The committee recommends action on national issues and the local land issue at Oka. The information provides an excellent example of First Nations-government relations.

Available from: Supply and Services Canada
Cost: $3

118

Martin, Fred V. "Federal and provincial responsibility in the Métis settlements of Alberta." In **Aboriginal peoples and government responsibility: Exploring federal and provincial roles,** edited by David C. Hawkes, 243-296. Ottawa: Carleton University Press, 1989.

Martin reports on the 1938 Métis Betterment Act of Alberta under which five geographic areas, approximately the size of P.E.I., were set aside for eight Métis settlements. Progress achieved and problems encountered over the past five decades are highlighted. Federal and provincial involvement, constitutional negotiations on recognition of rights of Métis, and the proposed 1988 Métis Settlement Act are reviewed.

Reading level: College
(FRE = 36   FI = 17   FK = 14)
Cost: $21.95

119

Opekokew, Delia. **The political and legal inequities among aboriginal peoples in Canada.** Kingston, ON: Institute of Intergovernmental Relations, Queen's University, 1987. 52 p.

This author examines the historical and legal background to aboriginal rights in Canada. She summarizes government policy as applied to the Inuit, Métis, status and non-status Indians, and treaty Indians, then presents the legal precedents for aboriginal rights. A brief overview of the Royal Proclamation and treaties is presented. The positions of the federal and provincial governments during the 1983-1987 constitutional negotiations are discussed and the positions of the four aboriginal groups are then reviewed.

Reading level: College
(FRE = 27   FI = 18   FK = 15)
Cost: $7

120

Point, Steven. "Understanding native activism." **B.C. Studies** 89 (Spring 1991): 124-129.

Point examines some milestones in history that negated native rights to self-determination and gave rise to longstanding anger and frustration. A rise in militancy suggests violence may become a means for resolving these outstanding issues. Point opposes violence and stresses the need for open, two-way communication between natives and governments. He concludes by outlining specific issues that both parties must clarify before communication can occur.

Reading level: Grade 12
(FRE = 43   FI = 16   FK = 12)
Cost: $10

121

Rawston, Bruce. "Federal perspectives on Indian-provincial relations." In **Governments in conflict? Provinces and Indian nations in Canada,** edited by J. Anthony Long and Menno Boldt, with Leroy Little Bear, 23-30. Toronto: University of Toronto Press, 1988.

Rawston, a deputy minister of Indian Affairs, discusses the federal government's current initiatives to encourage local government. His perspective is from the program and policy level.

Reading level: College
(FRE = 32   FI = 18   FK = 14)
Cost: $18.95

122

Scott, Ian G. "Respective roles and responsibilities of federal and provincial governments regarding the aboriginal peoples of Canada." In **Aboriginal peoples and government responsibility: Exploring federal and provincial roles,** edited by David C. Hawkes, 351-358. Ottawa: Carleton University Press, 1989.

Transcript of a speech by the former Minister of Aboriginal Affairs for Ontario. Mr. Scott discusses federal and provincial roles and responsibilities in providing services to aboriginal people. He notes that although aboriginal people are "citizens plus" in terms of rights, the opposite is true for access to services. He further suggests a new policy must be implemented with the federal government assuming responsibility for protecting and promoting "aboriginal" service components, and provincial governments assuming responsibility for equality of services.

Reading level: University
(FRE = 30   FI = 19   FK = 16)
Cost: $21.95

123

York, Geoffrey and Loreen Pindera. **People of the Pines: The warriors and the legacy of Oka.** Toronto: Little, Brown and Company Canada, 1991. 438 p.

The armed standoff between the Mohawk and the Canadian armed forces is described as the first domestic war since the Northwest Rebellion of 1885. This comprehensive account draws upon a variety of sources and is written by two reporters who covered the events from behind the barricades. It begins with a dramatic re-creation of the Surete du Quebec raid on July 11, 1990. Then, the authors recount the 270-year Mohawk struggle to protect their sovereignty and territory, and government inaction on their land claims. Events behind the barricades are described, as are the numerous negotiations and confrontations that occurred during the siege at Oka and the closure of the Mercier bridge. Recommended reading for those interested in gaining a better understanding of Mohawk land claims.

Reading level: Grade 11
(FRE = 55   FI = 15   FK = 11)
Cost: $29.95

Part II

Current Issues

Social issues

124

Assembly of First Nations. **The National Indian health transfer conference.** Ottawa: National Indian Brotherhood, 1988. 42 p.

This succinct report on the "First Nations' Government and Health Care" conference presents findings on the transfer of health services. Attendees believe health care is a basic human right and relate system failures to jurisdictional problems. Though many view the transfer policy as a threat more than an opportunity, many legitimate questions and concerns are raised. Numerous (85) recommendations identify current health concerns that extend beyond health transfer.

Reading level: College
(FRE = 24   FI = 20   FK = 17)
Available from: Assembly of First Nations
Cost: free

125

British Columbia. Premier's Council on Native Affairs. **Progress report and interim recommendations.** Victoria, B.C.: The Council, 1990. 16 p.

This interim report reviews government's aboriginal policies and consultations with First Nations. The Council reports on existing barriers to economic development for aboriginals, social problems encountered in communities, and the issue of aboriginal land claims.

Reading level: College
(FRE = 31   FI=18   FK=15)
Available from: Ministry of Native Affairs
Cost: free

126

B.C. Royal Commission on Health Care and Costs. "Native health." In **Closer to home: The report of the British Columbia Royal Commission on Health Care and Costs,** Vol. 2, C22-C33. Victoria, B.C.: B.C. Royal Commission on Health Care and Costs, 1991.

The Commission highlights health inequities among Indian people: lower life expectancy (15 years less) and higher infant mortality rates (3 times more). Inequality in service delivery and access to services is summarized. Health transfer problems are briefly discussed. Recommendations (17) include establishing a Native Health Branch.

Reading level: Grade 12
(FRE = 50   FI = 15   FK = 12)
Available from: Crown Publications
Cost: $28.50

127

Canada. Health and Welfare. **Health status of Canadian Indians and Inuit: Update 1987.** Ottawa: Indian and Northern Health Services, Medical Services Branch, 1988. 69 p.

A consultant summarizes health data on natives to 1985 and compares rates to those of the Canadian population in general. An infant mortality rate twice as high and suicide rate three to six times as high among Indian people clearly demonstrate health inequities in Canada. Topics include causes of death, major diseases, accidents, violence, and life-style factors that contribute to poor health. Many tables and graphs are used.

Reading Level: College
(FRE = 31   FI = 16   FK = 14)
Available from: library loan (out of print)

128

Comeau, Pauline. **The first Canadians: A profile of Canada's native people today.** Toronto: J. Lorimer, 1990. 170 p.

This book examines native issues during the two decades since the 1969 White Paper. The research, compiled by reporters of the *Winnipeg Free Press*, includes government reports obtained under the Freedom of Information Act as well as interviews with program administrators and First Nations' leaders. It presents a sympathetic portrayal of the difficulties encountered by First Nations with emphasis on Manitoba communities. Includes discussions on education, health, child welfare, justice, and self-government.

Reading level: Grade 12
(FRE = 45   FI = 16   FK = 12)
Cost: $13.95

129

Goldthorpe, W. G., Commissioner. **Report to the Minister, Indian health and health care: Alert Bay, B.C.** Ottawa: Health and Welfare, 1980. 63 p.

The tragic death of a 10-year-old girl triggered this inquiry into the health of 10 Nimpkish bands. Goldthorpe examines high death rates, briefly discusses health problems, and suggests that socio-economic factors are a contributing cause. Health, physician, and hospital services, and the role of Indian Affairs and Medical Services also explain poor health. He discusses the possibility of improving health by reviving Indian culture and makes 30 recommendations for change.

Reading Level: College
(FRE = 38   FI = 18   FK = 14)
Available from: library loan (out of print)

130

Hale, Janet Campbell. **Native students with problems of addiction.** Salmon Arm, B.C.: Native Adult Education Resource Centre, 1990. 205 p.

Native author Janet Campbell Hale and the NAERC prepared this book to provide information on preventing, identifying, and intervening in addictive behaviours. Many original activities are included to help native adults build self-esteem, set goals, provide peer counselling, develop positive Indian identity, confront issues affecting native people, and learn more about addictions. Resources and a list of alcohol and drug organizations and programs are provided. Produced by/for First Nations people.
Recommended and annotated by Don Sawyer, Native Adult Education Resource Centre.

Reading Level: Grade 8-10 (provided by annotator)
Cost: $13.50

131

Krotz, Larry. **Indian country inside another Canada.** Toronto: McClelland & Stewart, 1990. 254 p.

Personal observations and interviews in five communities across the country form the basis for this sympathetic portrayal of life on reserve. Experiences of the people of Cape Mudge, Norway House, Kanesatake, Tobique, and Onogaming reveal the commitment of community leaders and the challenges they face in trying to improve the conditions under which their people live.

Reading level: Grade 9
(FRE = 60   FI = 13   FK = 9)
Cost: $28.95

132

Prince George Native Friendship Centre. **PGNFC Newsletter.** (Quarterly) Prince George, B.C.: PGNFC.

The *PGNFC Newsletter* is for a targeted group of native/non-native people in the community and area of Prince George. It attempts to introduce the centre's programs to the general public and to provide a forum for those wishing to share their ideas. A future project may be to issue a literary art journal. Networking is an important part of this organization's mandate in delivering, implementing, and supporting programs at the PGNFC. Produced by/for First Nations people. *Recommended and annotated by Dan George, PGNFC.*

Reading Level: Grade 8 (provided by annotator)
Cost: shipping

133

Speck, Dara Culhane. **An error in judgement: The politics of medical care in an Indian/white community.** Vancouver: Talonbooks, 1987. 281 p.; photographs.

In 1979, an 11-year-old native girl died from an undiagnosed ruptured appendix while in the Alert Bay Hospital. This is a sensitive exploration of historical and political factors that created the environment for such a tragedy. Speck, a social activist and member of the Nimpkish Band, engages the reader in an exploration of racism and colonialism from the inside out and presents a clear case for the need for social and political change.

Reading Level: College
(FRE = 45   FI = 20   FK = 19)
Cost: $17.95

Child welfare

134
Richard Cardinal: Cry from a diary of a Métis child. Ottawa: National Film Board, 1986. 1/2" VHS videocassette; 29 minutes; colour; sound.

Child apprehension is considered one of the many attacks on the family and cultural life of native Canadians. This film is a tribute to Richard Cardinal, a Métis youth who committed suicide at the age of 17 after being shuffled through 28 foster homes. His death resulted in a judicial inquiry. The video provides useful background information for discussions on child welfare and cultural identity. *Teachers should preview* this video, as content is very distressing and may cause problems for some students.

Available from: Legal Resource Centre, Legal Services Society
Rental: free

135
Canada. Indian and Northern Affairs. **Adoption and the Indian child.** Ottawa: Supply and Services Canada, 1989. 39 p.

Lobbying and negotiations with the federal and provincial governments by native groups has led to improved sensitivity in dealing with the adoption of Indian children. This booklet is aimed at people who adopt Indian children. It gives basic information on the rights of Indian people and on tribes.

Reading Level: Grade 12
(FRE = 49   FI = 15   FK = 12)
Available from: Microlog 89 - 00305
Cost: $20

136
Canada. Child and Family Services Task Force. **Indian child and family services in Canada: Final report.** Ottawa: Indian and Northern Affairs, 1987. 61 p.

This report reviews existing data on child and family services for bands. A brief historical review of child welfare, child population statistics, and service agreements provides useful background. Numerous tables and bar graphs summarize service costs by region. This "limited" data base shows variations in service delivery costs and is intended to support decision making by planners and administrators.

Reading level: College
(FRE = 37   FI = 19   FK = 14)
Available from: Microlog 88 - 03000
Cost: $20

137
Carasco, Emily F. "Canadian native children: Have child welfare laws broken the circle?" **Canadian Journal of Family Law** 5(1) (Summer 1986): 111-138.

Carasco's review of child welfare legislation leads her to conclude that legislation discriminates against the native child. Complex arguments support her belief that insufficient focus on the "indigenous factor" dislocates the child from his/her culture and breaks the circle of life. System failures are due primarily to non-recognition of native culture and child care practices. Based on Ontario experiences.

Reading level: Grade 12
(FRE = 46   FI = 16   FK = 13)

138
Dumont, Reginald T. **Indian controlled child welfare: Adult survivors of child welfare stimulate their community to action.** Victoria, B.C.: Amicus Populi Consulting Ltd., 1991. 16 p.

Dumont personalizes the effects of policies in the 1950s and 1960s by using accounts of Indian people's experiences in boarding schools and in their villages. He evaluates the history of Spallumcheen Band's Child Welfare Program and uses transcript excerpts to highlight reactions of the authorities to the initiative. He offers a brief analysis of the stages in recognizing a social problem that precede community action.

Reading Level: Grade 12
(FRE = 39   FI = 17   FK = 13)
Available from: library loan (out of print)

139

Hepworth, H. Philip. **Foster care and adoption in Canada.** Ottawa: Canadian Council on Social Development, 1980. 243 p.; bibliography.

This long, dry document studies the operation of Child Welfare Services from 1959 to 1979. It chronicles escalating apprehensions of native children by provinces and relates this to changing social and demographic conditions. Numerous tables summarize data; statistics are quoted often. The author "interprets and presents" data and concludes by identifying several areas for future study.

Reading Level: Grade 12
(FRE = 45   FI = 16   FK = 13)
Cost: $11

140

Johnston, Patrick. **Native children and the child welfare system.** Toronto: J. Lorimer, 1983. 150 p.; bibliography.

Johnston's critical exposé presents the facts and background to the controversy surrounding native child welfare. He explains the jurisdictional tangle involved in the issue and presents current Canadian data on the treatment of native children within the system. A review of several initiatives by bands and organizations demonstrates new and promising developments in child welfare. Recommended reading.

Reading Level: College
(FRE = 34   FI = 18   FK = 14)
Cost: $9.95

141

MacDonald, John A. "The child welfare programme of the Spallumcheen Indian Band in British Columbia." In **The challenge of child welfare**, edited by Kenneth L. Levitt and Brian Wharf, 253-265. Vancouver: University of British Columbia Press, 1985.

A historical examination of the Spallumcheen program and its principal features includes a list of circumstances requiring band intervention and potential courses of action. The author compares and contrasts band by-laws with existing by-laws and speaks highly of band successes. However, he concludes that B.C. bands are unlikely to adopt this or any other model until the issue of self-government is resolved.

Reading Level: University
(FRE = 26   FI = 21   FK = 17)
Cost: $23

142

MacDonald, John A. **Child welfare and the Native Indian peoples of Canada.** Vol. 5. Windsor, ON: University of Windsor, 1985.

MacDonald re-explores the past and present of native child welfare with a special focus on B.C. He examines two child welfare models and concludes that the Manitoba Tripartite model offers greater potential for dealing with the problem than does the Spallumcheen model. He also concludes that Indian people require a strong economic base to support social programs, and he links this base to land claims resolution.

Reading Level: College
(FRE = 25   FI = 21   FK = 17)
Available from: library loan (out of print)

143

MacDonald, John A. "The Spallumcheen Indian Band by-law and its potential impact on native Indian child welfare policy in British Columbia." **Canadian Journal of Family Law** 4(1) (January 1983): 75-96.

MacDonald examines child welfare policy rationale and failures from 1950 to 1972. Positive but limited changes begin with the 1972 Berger Report and progress from a bold 1980 band by-law. A comparative analysis of existing by-laws questions the band's resource adequacy and legitimate authority. Though band action is recognized as a pilot project, the unresolved issue demonstrates the need for social and political reform.

Reading level: University

144

Novosedlik, Stephen G. "Native children: white law." **Perception: A Canadian Journal of Social Comment** 6(3) (January/February 1983): 27-29.

In this brief article of condemnation, the author claims child welfare legislation is discriminatory because interpretation of the law is culturally biased toward Euro-Canadians. A discussion of a Winnipeg child custody case demonstrates the value conflict. Approaches to reform include ensuring native participation and considering other cultural viewpoints when law is made and interpreted.

Reading Level: College
(FRE = 38   FI = 18   FK = 14)

145

Pimento, Barbara. **Native families in jeopardy: The child welfare system in Canada.** Toronto: Ontario Institute for Studies in Education, 1985. 17 p.

This analysis of native child welfare discusses the Canadian government's basis for service delivery. Tables summarize data for children in care during 1980-81, with cultural differences providing some explanation for existing problems. A discussion of possible solutions focuses on Ontario with the author concluding there is a need for training of native social workers and cross-cultural training.

Reading Level: College
(FRE = 31   FI = 17   FK = 15)

146

Ratner, R. S. **Child welfare services for urban Native Indians.** Vancouver: University of British Columbia Press, 1990. 66 p.

A consultant for United Native Nations re-examines service failures and analyzes factors contributing to higher rates of child apprehension in Vancouver. The need for better preventive services leads to discussion of four service delivery models. The consultant recommends a "unity" model, with UNN as co-ordinator, which enables parties with a vested interest to work together. The report concludes with an outline for a seven-year phasing-in process.

Reading Level: University
(FRE = 18   FI = 23   FK = 19)
Available from: library loan (out of print)

147

Sullivan, Terrence. "Native children in treatment: Clinical, social and cultural issues." **Journal of Child Care** 1(4) (May 1983): 75-94.

A Clinical Service Director for Youth provides another perspective on the history of native child welfare, but offers no new explanations for the deplorable statistics. He explores cultural differences in childrearing practices and mentions the much-quoted Spallumcheen initiative. Five case reports in the appendix provide a brief look at the human costs of putting a native child into non-native society.

Reading Level: College
(FRE = 41   FI = 17   FK = 15)

148

Ward, Margaret. **The adoption of native Canadian children.** Cobalt, ON: Highway Book Shop, 1984. 69 p.; bibliography.

The author studied problems in interracial adoptions between 1971 and 1978. The B.C. component of the study identifies a few program failures in placing native children in native homes. The researcher notes some problems in recruiting native adoptive homes and discusses a few promising initiatives for the future (e.g., adoption by custom).

Reading level: College
(FRE = 38   FI = 17   FK = 14)
Cost: $5.95

149

Wharf, Brian. **Toward First Nations control of child welfare: A review of emerging developments in B.C.** Victoria, B.C.: University of Victoria, December 1987.

This B.C. study explores new approaches to providing child welfare. Wharf starts with a lengthy discussion of existing problems in the child welfare system and traditional child care practices. He then discusses existing initiatives and related declines in children in care without first summarizing study findings. Two strategies are presented as ways to strengthen local child welfare efforts.

Reading level: University
(FRE = 16   FI = 26   FK = 22)
Available from: Social Planning and Research Council of B.C.
Cost: $4

150

Wuerscher, Rose. **Problems with the legislative base for native child welfare services.** Ottawa: Indian and Northern Affairs, 1979. 57 p.

This examination of the child welfare problem starts with a review of related policy. Many references to law and court cases show how the system fails to recognize the special needs of Indian people and the consequences of that failure. The author then reviews U.S. experiences and by comparison points to failures in the Canadian court system. Only brief mention is made of sensitizing legislation.

Reading level: Grade 12
(FRE = 45   FI = 17   FK = 13)
Available from: library loan (out of print)

Mask
made by R. Davidson

photo: Alexis MacDonald-Seto

Education

151

Assembly of First Nations. **Tradition and education: Towards a vision of our future.** 4 vols. Ottawa: The Assembly of First Nations, 1989.

This four-volume report represents the first Canada-wide position paper on education since NIB's *Indian Control of Indian Education* (1973). The report is based on four years of comprehensive community-based research. Findings are presented in four areas: jurisdiction, quality of education, management, and resourcing. The 54 recommendations present First Nations' positions on First Nations' control of education.

Reading level: University
(FRE = 8   FI = 22   FK = 18)
Cost: $50

152

Atleo, E. Richard. "A study of education in context." **B.C. Studies** 89 (Spring 1991): 104-119.

In this summary of a study done for his doctoral dissertation, Atleo applies his "theory of context" to examine internal and external factors affecting aboriginal educational achievements. The data support his hypothesis that improved educational achievements coincide with society's more positive attitudes toward natives. His summarized data is not easy to understand.

Reading level: Grade 12
(FRE = 43   FI = 17   FK = 12)
Cost: $10

153

Barman, Jean, Yvonne Hebert, and Don McCaskill, eds. **Indian education in Canada. Vol. 1, The legacy.** Vancouver: University of British Columbia Press, 1986. 167 p.

Eight painstakingly detailed essays provide an alternative interpretation of Indian education by whites and its role in the assimilation policy of the early 1900s. While the authors consider the policy to be abandoned today, they believe the underlying "Indian problem" remains undefined. In their exploration of failures, inconsistencies, and cruelties of past policies, they conclude that the legacy of these policies is a problem that needs to be addressed today. Arguments are interesting but complex.

Reading level: Grade 12
(FRE=41   FI = 17   FK = 13)
Cost: $17.95

154

Barman, Jean, Yvonne Hebert, and Don McCaskill, eds. **Indian education in Canada. Vol. 2, The challenge.** Vancouver: University of British Columbia Press, 1986. 252 p.; bibliography.

The 12 articles by First Nations' educators, scholars, and practitioners examine the changes in education since the 1972 "Indian Control of Indian Education" position paper. Diane Longboat gives a historical and legislative perspective of First Nations' control of education and assesses progress achieved since 1972. Individual chapters are case studies of community experiences in assuming control of education. Of particular interest are papers on two First Nations' controlled school boards. Billy Diamond discusses difficulties encountered with the federal and provincial governments; Alvin Mckay and Bert Mckay discuss challenges encountered in implementing their bilingual-bicultural education program. Also of interest are chapters discussing teacher training in Mount Currie. Two case studies on Mi'kmaq literacy and the Blue Quills Education Centre are continuations from Volume 1.

Reading level: Grade 12
(FRE = 36   FI = 16   FK = 12)
Cost: $19.50

155

Barman, Jean. "Separate and unequal: Indian and white girls at All Hallows School, 1884-1920." In **Indian education in Canada. Vol. 1, The legacy.** Edited by Jean Barman, Yvonne Hebert, and Don McCaskill, 110-131. Vancouver: University of British Columbia Press, 1986.

Prior to 1900, Indian and white girls at an Anglican boarding school are separated at work and play but equal in studies. After 1900, inequality extends to the classroom and derives from prejudice and deliberately restricted federal funding. Barman believes this case explains how reversal of the assimilation policy succeeded in maintaining the social order of the time, the effects of which are still seen today.

Reading level: Grade 12
(FRE = 43   FI = 16   FK = 12)
Cost: $17.95

156

Canada. Employment and Immigration, Aboriginal Employment and Training Working Group. **Pathways to success: Aboriginal employment and training strategy.** 2 vols. Ottawa: Public Affairs, Employment and Immigration Canada, 1991. 22 p.; illus.

In 1989 Employment and Immigration Canada (EIC) announced a new labour force development strategy. The Aboriginal Employment and Training Working Group was established as part of the new initiative in response to aboriginal concerns about extremely high rates of aboriginal unemployment and the untrained aboriginal workforce. This publication is the group's report of their review of EIC's policies, programs, and services. In Volume 1, the committee examines current programs and services and notes levels of use by aboriginal people and the problems they encounter. In Volume 2, "A Policy and Implementation Paper," a new partnership is proposed based on five principles relating to consultation, delivery and funding mechanisms, employment equity, and eligibility for services. Six appendices detail management and operational issues.

Reading level: College
(FRE = 27   FI = 20   FK=16)
Cost: free

157

Canada. House of Commons, Standing Committee on Aboriginal Affairs. **You took my talk: Aboriginal literacy and empowerment.** Ottawa: The Committee, 1990. 139 p.

The United Nations General Assembly declared 1990 International Literacy Year to encourage member countries to examine literacy and create a plan to reduce if not eradicate illiteracy. Illiteracy among aboriginal people is estimated to be three times that of the general Canadian population. This report considers both official and aboriginal language literacy. Briefs received by the committee from First Nations point to funding shortages due to federal/provincial jurisdictional disputes; lack of adequate facilities; and lack of culturally appropriate education programs. The report includes committee and First Nations recommendations for improving access to literacy.

Reading level: College
(FRE = 17   FI = 20   FK = 16)
Available from: Supply and Services Canada
Cost: $10

158

Crey, Ernie. "The children of tomorrow's great potlatch." **B.C. Studies** 89 (Spring 1991): 150-158.

Crey discusses education within the context of residential schools and child apprehension. He describes the devastating effects on individuals, families, and communities and parallels natives reclaiming lost children with reclaiming their rightful place in Canadian society. The potlatch symbolizes his hope for the future, where natives and non-natives create solutions to problems in harmony.

Reading level: Grade 11
(FRE = 57   FI = 14   FK = 11)
Cost: $10

159

Gresko, Jacqueline. "Creating little dominions within the Dominion: Early Catholic schools in Saskatchewan and British Columbia." In **Indian education in Canada. Vol 1, The legacy**, edited by Jean Barman, Yvonne Hebert, and Don McCaskill, 88-103. Vancouver: University of British Columbia Press, 1986.

This scholarly article compares Cree and Stalo responses to the 1860 Catholic residential school. Gresko describes roles and routines and shows how the native people successfully resist assimilation by coupling traditional practices with public school events. She finds it puzzling that both peoples adapt and retain components of the system that conform with their past and current needs.

Reading level: Grade 12
(FRE = 45   FI = 16   FK = 12)
Cost: $17.95

160
Haig-Brown, Celia. **Resistance and renewal: Surviving the Indian residential school.** Vancouver: Tillacum Library, 1988. 158 p.; photographs; bibliography.

Invasion and resistance are central themes in this report of interviews with 13 former students of the Kamloops Indian Residential School. Numerous quotes create an emotional portrayal of life in a residential school and the system's effects on family life before and after. Despite personal pain, we see emerging a picture of a strong people and a strong culture growing, adapting, and surviving.

Reading level: Grade 10
(FRE = 59   FI = 13   FK = 10)
Cost: $11.95

161
MacPherson, James C. **MacPherson report on tradition and education: Towards a vision of our future.** Ottawa: Indian Affairs and Northern Development, 1991. 45 p.

This study was commissioned by Indian Affairs in response to the Assembly of First Nations' report "Tradition and education: Towards a vision of our future." MacPherson considers jurisdictional issues in implementing recommendations in the AFN report. He offers an historical overview and considers the current system of Indian education. Native education in other countries is briefly discussed. The constitutional framework of First Nations education is examined in detail, as is education as an aboriginal and treaty right. Four models of First Nations' control are considered. He makes eight recommendations supporting First Nations' control, including enactment of a national Indian education law.

Reading level: University
(FRE = 35   FI = 18   FK = 15)
Cost: free

162
Paquette, Jerry. **Aboriginal self-government in education in Canada.** Kingston, ON: Institute of Intergovernmental Relations, Queen's University, 1986. 120 p.; bibliography.

Many people consider First Nations' control of education to be a critical component of self-government. This report examines issues involved in self-government in education and identifies a number of alternatives on how this may be achieved. The current structure of administration, financing, and policy development is examined. Resourcing issues are considered. A number of options are suggested at the national, provincial, regional, and local levels; the feasibility and potential for political support of each one is examined.

Reading level: University
(FRE = 14   FI = 20   FK = 17)
Cost: $10

163
Rodriguez, Carmen, and Don Sawyer. **Native literacy research report.** Salmon Arm, B.C.: Native Adult Education Resource Centre (for the Ministry of Advanced Education, Province of B.C. and Multi-culturalism and Citizenship, Canada), 1990. 113 p.

This B.C. study examines the serious problem of illiteracy, using a survey of 56 potential literacy native adult learners. The survey covers the purpose and perceived value of literacy, past barriers to learning to read and write, positive learning environment, and current barriers to participation.

Reading level: College
(FRE = 38   FI = 17   FK = 15)
Cost: $10.10

Criminal justice

164

"Native people's access to justice." **Legal Perspectives** 14(4) (May 1990).

The May 1990 issue of *Legal Perspectives* is written and illustrated primarily by native lawyers and students. It covers a variety of topics including such legal issues as Indian government, adoption, and education. The emphasis is on Indians in the justice system.

Reading level: Grade 12
(FRE = 47   FI = 15   FK = 12)
Available from: Schools Program, Legal Services Society
Cost: free

165

Cowan, Paul. **Justice denied.** Ottawa: National Film Board of Canada, 1989. Film or videocassette; 98 minutes; colour; sound.

This is an account of one of the most tragic and publicized cases of racism in the Canadian judicial system. The film documents the story of Donald Marshall, Jr., a Micmac Indian who was charged with and served 11 years for a murder he did not commit. An inquiry into the judicial system results in 82 recommendations for improvement.

Cost: $34.95

166

B.C. Ministries of Solicitor General, Attorney General, and Native Affairs. **Native justice consultations: Progress report and action plan.** Victoria, B.C.: Queen's Printer, 1990. 33 p.

This brief, glossy report summarizes the discoveries of a first round of consultation in B.C. It describes and analyzes the strengths and weaknesses of the process; identifies key issues and common themes revealed through discussion; and outlines local responses to current initiatives. Five goals in the proposed action plan focus on changes to make the system more accessible, relevant, and responsive to natives.

Reading level: University
(FRE = 10   FI = 26   FK = 22)
Available from: Microlog 91 - 00157
Cost: $20

167

Canada. Solicitor General. **Final report: Task force on aboriginal peoples in federal corrections.** Ottawa: Supply and Services Canada, 1989. 109 p.

A committee examined the process of incarceration and possible means to socially re-integrate aboriginal offenders. Their report reviews justice mandates, policies, and programs and services within the context of the specific needs of aboriginals. Issues, recommendations (46), and strategies for change focus largely on the need to revise the structure of the justice system.

Reading level: University
(FRE = 20   FI = 22   FK = 18)
Available from: Microlog 91 - 05984
Cost: $30

168

Canadian Bar Association. Committee on Aboriginal Rights in Canada. **Report of the Canadian Bar Association Committee on Aboriginal Rights in Canada: An agenda for action.** Ottawa: Canadian Bar Association, 1988. 111 p.

The Canadian Bar Association established a native justice committee in 1986 in response to concerns that aboriginal people suffer injustices for which the legal system is responsible. Issues examined by the committee include treaties, aboriginal rights and title, self-government, and aboriginal people and the justice system. Alternative dispute mechanisms are examined and the advantages and disadvantages of negotiation versus litigation considered. The committee made 30 major recommendations on initiatives to recognize the special legal position of aboriginal people and to provide equity in the justice system.

Reading level: Grade 12
(FRE = 39   FI = 15   FK = 12)
Cost: $12

169

Clark, G. S., and Associates Ltd. **Native victims in Canada: Issues in providing effective assistance.** (No. 1986-50) Ottawa: Solicitor General of Canada, 1986. 88 p.; bibliography.

This study of the needs of native victims of crime takes into account the different perceptions natives have of crime and punishment. Three case studies are presented to illustrate this, including a Gitksan lawsuit. The report recommends that victim assistance programs be community-based and proposes that four pilot projects be done in urban and rural areas.

Reading level: College
(FRE = 40   FI = 18   FK = 15)
Available from: library loan (out of print)

170

Clark, Scott. **The Mi'kmaq and criminal justice in Nova Scotia: Research study prepared for the Royal Commission on the Donald Marshall, Jr., prosecution.** Vol 3. Halifax: The Commission, 1989. 109 p.

This report first examines issues affecting all Canadian aboriginal people, then focuses on the Mi'kmaq people and related structural failures in the criminal justice system. The 20 recommendations for change are wide in scope and include addressing socio-economic factors that contribute to the Mi'kmaq situation and developing a Mi'kmaq justice system. The report represents the researcher's views.

Reading level: College
(FRE = 24   FI = 21   FK = 17)
Available from: Microlog 90 - 02810
Cost: $30

Bird rattle
Gitksan

photo: Bill McLennan

171

Corrigan, Samuel W., and Lawrence J. Barkwell. **The struggle for recognition: Canadian justice and the Métis nation.** Winnipeg: Pemmican Publications, 1991. 219 p.; bibliography.

The research of the authors documents the struggle of the Métis people to retain and develop their own legal system. Analysis of injustices shows how the judicial system has failed the Métis (and Indian) people and how the system could be reformed to support current quests for self-determination.

Reading level: Grade 12
(FRE = 41   FI = 16   FK = 13)
Cost: $19.95 (paperback); $27.95 (hardbound)

172

Depew, Robert. **Native policing in Canada: A review of current issues.** Ottawa: Solicitor General of Canada, 1986. 169 p.; bibliography.

This long, well-researched report includes "troubling" provincial data relevant to B.C. Review of an exhaustive range of related issues chops up the report. An examination of existing tribal initiatives and types of offences lead Depew to conclude there may be a need to redefine relationships with the criminal justice system. He identifies areas for further research.

Reading level: University
(FRE = 12   FI = 22   FK = 20)
Available from: Microlog 87 - 05694
Cost: $30

173

Fearn, Lorraine, and George Kupfer. **A program review and evaluation assessment — criminal courtworkers: Native counselling services of Alberta.** Ottawa: Department of Justice, 1981. 205 p.

Includes a lengthy description of services, a summary of the views of numerous natives regarding each service, and an examination of the availability of data on native offences and processing in the system. An evaluation model is proposed. Potential research questions and study variables are suggested. Useful research facts.

Reading level: Grade 11
(FRE = 51   FI = 14   FK = 11)
Available from: library loan (out of print)

174

Gitksan-Wet'suwet'en Education Society, Smithers Indian Friendship Centre, Upper Skeena Counselling and Legal Assistance Society. **Unlocking aboriginal justice: Alternative dispute resolution for the Gitksan and Wet'suwet'en people.** 1989. 56 p. Phase 1 Resubmission (1990) 13 p. Photocopied.

Inadequacies and failures of the justice system led to this proposal for an alternative system based on cultural dispute-resolution laws and methods. The concepts are developed from an extensive examination of traditional values and practices and are integrated into the provincial justice system. This three-year project focuses on education and is intended to be self-supporting at project completion.

Reading level: University
(FRE = 28   FI = 22   FK = 18)
Available from: Office of the Hereditary Chiefs of the Gitksan and Wet'suwet'en
Cost: photocopying cost

175

Griffiths, Curt Taylor, ed. **Preventing and responding to northern crime.** Vancouver: Simon Fraser University and the Northern Justice Society, 1989. 288 p.

Summarizes the presentations (including question periods) of reports by 25 individuals and organizations from across Canada at a conference on northern crime. Although presenters discuss local justice problems and strategies for dealing with them, the issues are relevant to most aboriginal communities in Canada.

Reading level: Grade 8
(FRE = 62   FI = 11   FK = 8)
Available from: Northern Justice Society
Cost: $35

176

Hartman, D. M., A. D. Kirkaldy, G. K. Muirhead, and A. G. Law. **Analysis of native Indian admissions to the B.C. correctional system for 1975.** Victoria, B.C.: B.C. Corrections Branch, Ministry of the Attorney-General, 1976. 96 p.

In 1975 natives accounted for 13.5% of all admissions to the corrections system and less than 2% of the general population. This descriptive study discounts structural problems and explains over-representation in terms of high rural distribution, high rates of seasonal migration, absence of a cash economy, and minority labelling. Many confusing tables compare provincial and regional data according to native/non-native status. No overall conclusion is drawn.

Reading level: College
(FRE = 18   FI = 20   FK = 16)
Available from: library loan (out of print)

177

Havemann, Paul, Lori Foster, Keith Couse, and Rae Matonovich. **Law and order for Canada's indigenous people.** Ottawa: Solicitor General of Canada, 1984. 187 p.; bibliography.

This detailed working paper assesses Canadian research literature between 1972 and 1983 and describes the impact of parts of the criminal justice system on indigenous people. The authors relate over-representation in the system to colonization and under-development and suggest this will remain a problem until socio-economic issues are resolved. The report contains numerous quotes from literature.

Reading level: College
(FRE = 17   FI = 22   FK = 17)
Available from: Microlog 85 - 03368
Cost: $30

178

Horn, Charles, and Curt Taylor Griffiths. **Native North Americans: Crime, conflict and criminal justice; A research bibliography.** 4th ed. Burnaby, B.C.: Northern Justice Society, 1989.

An excellent bibliography arranged by subject and covering journal articles, government publications, and unpublished papers. It contains materials primarily on criminal justice and related fields (community life, Constitution, civil liberties, education, Indian Act, administration of justice, adult offenders, juvenile delinquency, etc.). Out of print, but being updated.

Reading level: Grade 12
(FRE = 26   FI = 16   FK = 13)
Available from: library loan (out of print)

179

Jackson, Michael. **Locking up natives in Canada: A report of the committee of the Canadian Bar Association on imprisonment and release.** Vancouver: University of British Columbia Press, June 1988. 110 p.

This report uses shocking comparisons to draw attention to native over-representation in Canadian prisons. It explores aboriginal courts in three countries and compares them to Canadian initiatives in dealing with the problem. Jackson concludes that a separate aboriginal justice system is a viable and necessary option for providing justice to natives. Legalese is used extensively.

Reading level: University
(FRE = 23   FI = 24   FK = 19)
Available from: library loan (out of print)

180

Lapraire, Carol, and Barbara Craig. **Native criminal justice research and programs: An inventory.** Ottawa: Solicitor General of Canada, 1984. 188 p.

This report inventories research and programming activities related to native people and criminal justice in Canada. Some programs may now be inactive due to short-term funding. Topics include diversion, policing, and involvement of natives in the criminal justice system as practitioners. The inventory includes a description of the activity, funding sources, and a contact person's address. An update was published in 1987.

Reading level: Grade 11
(FRE = 47   FI = 15   FK = 11)
Available from: Microlog 85 - 03369
Cost: $30

181

Law Reform Commission of Canada. **Report on aboriginal peoples and criminal justice: Equality, respect and the search for justice.** Ottawa: Law Reform Commission of Canada, 1991. 111 p.

The Commission consults with aboriginal peoples (who want action and not further study) as it seeks to propose reforms to offset results of a history of disadvantage and suffering within the system. An impartial reporting of failures leads to many short- and long-term recommendations for change. Short-term proposals are for fixing up the existing system; the most contentious long-term proposal is to establish a parallel aboriginal justice system.

Reading level: University
(FRE = 16   FI = 21   FK = 18)
Cost: free

182

Manitoba. Aboriginal Justice Inquiry. **Report of the Aboriginal Justice Inquiry of Manitoba/Public inquiry into the administration of justice and aboriginal people.** Winnipeg: The Inquiry, 1991. 2 vols. Vol. 1, The justice system and aboriginal people. Vol. 2, The deaths of Helen Betty Osborne and John Joseph Harper.

The Aboriginal Justice Inquiry was created in response to public outcry over the deaths of Betty Osborne and John Joseph Harper, and subsequent treatment of the incidents by the justice system. The inquiry held extensive public hearings and did technical research to consider all components of the justice system including policing; access and adequacy to legal counsel; court processes; court dispositions and sentencing; awareness of the justice system; and communication and employment of aboriginal people in the system.

Although the inquiry deals with issues in Manitoba, conditions reflect those of all native people. This is an important reference for the study of native justice.

Volume 1 examines aboriginal people in the justice system. An historical overview emphasizes aboriginal rights and treaties, the reasons for over-representation in prisons, and the role of systemic discrimination. Recommendations are made for improving the justice system, including establishing a separate justice system for aboriginal people.

Volume 2 examines the deaths of Betty Osborne and John Joseph Harper and the investigations of the deaths, including the actions of the community and the legal system. The inquiry found racism to be at the root of these events. Recommendations are made for improving the responsiveness of the system.

A summary of Volume 1 is available on videocassette in English, Cree, Ojibway, Dene, Dakota, and Island Lake.

Reading level: College
(FRE = 28   FI = 20   FK = 14)
Available from: Queen's Printer, Manitoba
Cost: $20

183

Mannette, J. A. "Not being a part of the way things work: Tribal culture and systemic exclusion in the Donald Marshall Inquiry." **Canadian Review of Sociology and Anthropology** 27(4) (1990): 505-529.

Mannette says the Marshall Inquiry operated in a culturally biased environment which excluded the Micmac world view. However, as he ably shows, the inquiry does provide an opportunity for learning about Micmac values and practices. Many ethnographic theories are presented and supported by quotes from scholars and testimony from Micmac people.

Reading level: College
(FRE = 19   FI = 21   FK = 16)
Available from: University of Guelph/University Microfilms

184

Moran, Bridget. **Judgement at Stoney Creek.** Vancouver: Arsenal Pulp Press, 1990.

This story provides an example of the racism and major shortcomings found in the criminal justice system in British Columbia. Moran reveals the hit-and-run death of a young, pregnant Carrier woman from Stoney Creek. A detailed presentation of the actions of the native and non-native communities following the event leaves the reader feeling that the grief and pain continue today.

Reading level: Grade 10
(FRE = 63   FI = 13   FK = 10)
Cost: $12.95

185

Nova Scotia. Royal Commission on the Donald Marshall, Jr., Prosecution. **Royal Commission on the Donald Marshall, Jr., Prosecution. Commissioners' report: Findings and recommendations.** Vol. 1. Halifax: The Commission, 1989. 406 p.

Prior to conducting an inquiry into the wrongful conviction of a Micmac man, the Royal Commission first sets out to determine the facts surrounding the case. Adequacy of and process for compensation to Marshall and the general issue of racism also receive attention. This introspective report poses numerous questions and makes 82 recommendations for change. Findings are well summarized.

Reading level: Grade 11
(FRE = 55   FI = 14   FK = 11)
Available from: Microlog 90 - 02822
Cost: $55

Environmental protection

186
Blockade: Algonquins defend the forest. Ottawa: National Film Board of Canada, 1990. Film or videocassette; 27 minutes; colour; sound.

As with many Indian people in North America, the Algonquin Indians of Quebec have powerlessly watched their homelands being decimated by clear-cut logging. In September 1989, a small group of Indian people challenged the government and logging industry by setting up a blockade to save their lands. This Quebec experience has many parallel situations in B.C.

Cost: $26.95
Rental: $5/week

187
Hunters and bombers. Ottawa: National Film Board of Canada, 1990. Film or videocassette; 53 minutes; colour; sound.

For nearly a decade, the Innu people of Labrador have been attempting to stop the low-level flying of NATO jet bombers over their lands. The Innu believe the practice is detrimental to the animals, the environment, and their culture. This film also includes the concerns of the military, environmentalists, and peace groups.

Cost: $26.95

188
Ashini, Daniel. "David confronts Goliath: The Innu of Ungaga versus the NATO Alliance." In **Drumbeat: Anger and renewal in Indian country**, edited by Boyce Richardson, 45-70. Toronto: Summerhill Press, 1989.

Canada and the NATO alliance planned up to 40,000 low-level military training flights a year over Innu land by 1992. This article explains the impact on the Innu's traditional life-style and their resistance to the intrusion. Protecting their territory, called Nitassinan, is seen as fundamental to maintaining their culture.

Reading level: Grade 11
(FRE = 54   FI = 15   FK = 11)
Cost: $14.95

189
Flooding Job's garden. Ottawa: National Film Board of Canada, 1991. Film or videocassette; 57 minutes; colour; sound.

In 1975, the Quebec government forced through the James Bay and Northern Quebec Agreement to make way for a massive hydro-electric development. This land claims agreement brought numerous changes to the Cree people and their communities. This film documents the changes and the renewed fight to stop Premier Bourassa's plans for Phase 2 of the project.

Cost: $26.95
Rental: $5/week

190
Goldstick, Miles. **Wollaston: People resisting genocide.** Montreal: Black Rose Books, 1987. 311 p.; photographs.

Residents of a Chipewyan village take action to protect their homes and the environment from uranium mining in northern Saskatchewan. Goldstick, an environmental activist, documents events before, during, and after a blockade. He contrasts Indian and white relationships with the earth, reports individual responses, and discusses the harmful effects of uranium and its by-products. He includes poems as well as transcripts from interviews and meetings.

Reading level: Grade 9
(FRE = 56   FI = 12   FK = 9)
Cost: $16.95 (paperback); $36.95 (hardbound)

191

Haida Gwaii: Council of the Haida Nation. **Yakoun: River of life.** Masset, Haida Gwaii: Council of the Haida Nation, 1990. 40 p.; illus.

The Yakoun River on Haida Gwaii is being threatened by the development of an open-pit gold mine, logging of the river's basin and corridor, and a new pulp mill at Port Clements. Haida and non-Haida residents oppose these developments and have produced this booklet as their "effort to share the Yakoun in pictures, articles and stories and to show you, the reader, what we all stand to lose." Haida elders share their past, and the Haida youth share their elders' teachings. Beautifully illustrated.

Reading level: Grade 9
(FRE = 61   FI = 12   FK = 9)
Cost: $10.95 (all proceeds go to protect the river)

192

Harding, James. **Aboriginal rights and government wrongs: Uranium mining and neo-colonialism in northern Saskatchewan.** Regina: Prairie Justice Research, University of Regina, 1988. 43 p.

Harding assesses the government process inquiring into the advisability of mining radioactive minerals in northern Saskatchewan. He highlights aboriginal people's position regarding treaty and aboriginal rights and discusses their request for a moratorium on mining. He examines the inquiry board's mandate, which failed to consider First Nations' views. Harding argues that these actions are colonialist; he says development must take into account the rights of First Nations.

Reading level: College
(FRE = 30   FI = 19   FK = 15)
Cost: $5

193

Keeping, Janet M. **The Inuvialuit Final Agreement.** Calgary: Canadian Institute of Resources Law, 1989. 160 p.

Keeping examines the impact of the Inuvialuit Final Agreement on oil and gas explorations in the Northwest Territories. She summarizes sections of the agreement relating to mineral exploration and discusses the legal aspects of implementation legislation, the status of the agreement under section 35 of the Constitution, and the Charter of Rights. The report demonstrates the complexities of natural resource planning and environmental protection in comprehensive land claims agreements.

Reading level: University
Cost: $24

194

Linton, Jamie. "The geese have lost their way." **Nature Canada** (Spring 1991): 27-33.

A report on the impact of the James Bay hydro-electric dam on the Cree town of Chisasibi. Linton notes that "the rivers are the foundation of traditional Cree economy; by flooding the land the Quebec government has turned the lives of the Cree upside down." Interviews with native people illustrate the devastation of the traditional culture and the people's dissatisfaction with life in the "instant" towns.

Reading level: Grade 7
(FRE = 71   FI = 10   FK=7)
Available from: Canadian Nature Federation

195

M'Gonigle, Michael. "Developing sustainability: A native/environmentalist prescription for third-level government." **B.C. Studies** 84 (Winter 1989/90): 65-99.

The author argues for restructuring government to promote development that is sustainable and environmentally sound. Using the movement to save the Stein River valley as an example, he considers initiatives of native and environmental groups. He concludes that both will achieve their goals under a "third order of government that is locally controlled." He says that the two groups must work together more closely in order to achieve the needed change in government decision-making processes.

Reading level: College
(FRE = 22   FI = 21   FK = 17)
Cost: $10

196
M'Gonigle, Michael, and Wendy Wickwire. **Stein: The way of the river.** Vancouver: Talonbooks, 1988. 192 p.; illus.; maps.

The struggle to preserve the Stein River valley wilderness received national and international attention during the late 1980s. This book dramatically illustrates the argument for preservation by using archival photographs, excerpts from historical documents, environmental reports, interviews with native elders, and exceptional photographs. The culture and history of the Nlaka'pamux people is presented, followed by a description of the habitat. An overview of the area's development during the past century concludes with the conflicts that have developed and the emergence of the movement to the save the Stein. An argument is made for better resource use and planning that will protect wilderness areas such as the Stein.

Reading level: Grade 11
(FRE = 55   FI = 15   FK=11)
Cost: $39.95

197
Reed, Maureen G., Canadian Environmental Assessment Research Council. **Environmental assessment and aboriginal claims: Implementation of the Inuvialuit Final Agreement.** Ottawa: Canadian Environmental Assessment Research Council, [1990]. 67 p.; illus.; maps.

In 1984 the Inuvialuit of the western Arctic signed an agreement surrendering aboriginal title in exchange for compensation and management and ownership rights to 91 000 km² of land. This report examines the impact of clauses in the agreement dealing with environmental assessment procedures. The federal process and the new joint management process are compared. Although the joint process is considered a positive step in promoting local involvement in decision making, a number of questions are raised about the operation of this review process.

Reading level: College
(FRE = 34   FI = 18   FK = 14)
Cost: free

198
The Alliance of Tribal Nations. **The river is our home.** Vancouver: The Alliance of Tribal Nations, 1984. 3/4" videocassette; 34 minutes; colour; sound.

The Stalo, Nlaka'pamux, and Lillooet Nations of the Alliance of Tribal Nations present their concern over the proposed Canadian National Railways' plans to twin track along the Fraser River. They are concerned about the environmental impact and its effect upon Indian lands and fishing grounds.

Available from Legal Resource Centre, Legal Services Society
Rental: free

199
Waldram, James Burgess. **As long as the rivers run: Hydro-electric development and native communities in western Canada.** Winnipeg: University of Manitoba Press, 1988. 256 p.; maps; bibliography.

Waldram examines parallels between historic treaty-making and negotiations done as part of hydro-electric developments (that is, alienation of aboriginal land for the "common good"). Three case studies (Cumberland House and the Squaw Valley Rapids Dam; Esterville and the Grand Rapids Dam; South Indian Lake and the Churchill River diversion project) illustrate his point. The cases are based on government and First Nations reports and correspondence and interviews with the officials involved.

Reading level: College
(FRE = 34   FI = 21   FK = 17)
Cost: $24.95

Constitution

200

Dancing around the table. Ottawa: National Film Board of Canada, 1987. 2 films or videocassettes; Part 1: 57 minutes; Part 2: 50 minutes; colour; sound.

In Part 1, First Nations' leaders present their well-articulated concerns about the Constitution, aboriginal rights, and treaty rights at First Ministers' Constitutional Conferences in 1983, 1984, and 1985. Part 2 covers the fourth conference held in 1987. Recommended not only for its coverage of this important topic but also for its revelations about political morality and Indian versus non-Indian government relations.

Available from: Legal Resource Centre, Legal Services Society
Rental: free
Available from: National Film Board
Rental: $5/week

201

Assembly of Manitoba Chiefs. "Selected documents from the Assembly of Manitoba Chiefs on the Meech Lake Accord." **Native Studies Review** 6(1) (1990): 119-152.

Elijah Harper's blockage of the Meech Lake Accord in the Manitoba legislature was the culmination of three years of lobbying effort by the Assembly of Manitoba Chiefs. The 12 documents recording this period begin with the 1987 draft document entitled "Analysis of the potential impact of the Meech Lake Accord on the rights of aboriginal people." Other documents include internal letters, press releases explaining AMC's position, and a letter from Prime Minister Mulroney to the Manitoba chiefs. Phil Fontaine's and Elijah Harper's speeches to gatherings at the legislature building complete the collection.

Reading level: College
(FRE = 28   FI = 20   FK = 16)

202

Canada. Royal Commission on Aboriginal Peoples. **The right of aboriginal self-government and the Constitution: A commentary of the Royal Commission on Aboriginal Peoples.** Ottawa: The Commission, 1992. 37 p.; bibliography.

The Royal Commission expresses concern about an impasse in constitutional negotiations. The Commission proposes avenues to achieve constitutional entrenchment of self-government. Following an examination of the historical and legal background issues, the Commission states six criteria for successful reform. Four alternative approaches are also presented for consideration by all parties.

Reading level: College
(FRE = 24   FI = 20   FK = 16)
Cost: free

203

Canada. The Special Joint Committee on a Renewed Canada. **Aboriginal peoples, self-government, and constitutional reform.** Ottawa: Supply and Services Canada, 1991. 25 p.

This booklet provides background information on aboriginal issues for constitutional discussions. A brief overview on aboriginal people is followed by a summary of the legislative framework and policy initiatives of the federal government. The paper identifies issues to be addressed in negotiations and the federal government's position on the matter. (Note that since September 1991 the federal position on aboriginal self-government has become somewhat more flexible due to public pressure.)

Reading level: College
(FRE = 20   FI=19   FK=15)
Available from: Indian Affairs and Northern Development
Cost: free

204

Clark, Bruce A. **Native liberty, crown sovereignty: The existing aboriginal right of self-government in Canada.** Montreal: McGill-Queen's University Press, 1990. 259 p.; bibliography.

Clark argues that self-government has always existed in constitutional law. He uses exhaustive judicial and legislative research to support his argument that "the right was confirmed under legislation enacted by the imperial government, which has never been repealed, and it has been endorsed by constitutionally binding common law precedents." He further argues that problems arise when those charged with applying the law have chosen to ignore or misinterpret the law. Clark finds this disregard beginning with the colonial "segregation to integration" philosophy in the Indian Act. He offers suggestions on how to rectify this in future constitutional negotiations.

Reading level: College
(FRE = 26   FI = 20   FK = 16)
Cost: $39.95

205

Hall, Tony. "What are we? Chopped liver? Aboriginal affairs in the constitutional politics of Canada in the 1980s." In **Meech Lake primer: Conflicting views of the 1987 constitutional accord**, edited by Michael D. Behiels, 423-456. Ottawa: University of Ottawa Press, 1989.

Hall traces aboriginal people's efforts to have the right to self-government entrenched in the Constitution. He begins with repatriation and First Nations' lobbying the British House of Commons in 1981 and concludes with the lobbying initiative opposing the 1987 Meech Lake Accord. He argues that the federal government continually abdicated its responsibility to First Nations in order to get the premiers' consensus on other issues under negotiation. The paper gives insight into the political manoeuvring surrounding entrenchment of self-government.

Reading level: Grade 12
(FRE = 41   FI = 16   FK = 12)
Cost: $39.95

206

Hawkes, David Craig. **Aboriginal peoples and constitutional reform: What have we learned?** Kingston, ON: Institute of Intergovernmental Relations, Queen's University, 1989. 72 p.

This report represents the final phase of the institute's research on aboriginal constitutional issues. It critically examines the process of constitutional negotiations on aboriginal issues in light of the failure to reach consensus in 1987. The structure, the issues raised, and the negotiations are assessed by using verbatim transcripts of the 1987 constitutional conference, media reports, and personal interviews with 12 of the 17 participants. Problems are discussed in order to apply lessons learned to future negotiations. The Meech Lake Accord is also assessed.

Reading level: College
(FRE = 31   FI = 18   FK = 14)
Cost: $21.95

207

Matchewan, Jean Maurice. "Will Quebec recognize distinct native society?" In **Visions of Canada: Disparate views of what Canada is, what it ought to be, and what it might become**, edited by Earle Grey, 59-61. Woodville, ON: Canadian Speeches, 1990.

This May 3, 1990 speech to a committee of the House of Commons is by the Algonquin Chief of Barriere Lake in Quebec. He states the Algonquin position on the Meech Lake Accord, describes relations with the Quebec government and argues that Canada is obligated to protect the rights of First Nations in Quebec. The speech provides insight into complex issues involved in the planned Quebec referendum on separation from Canada.

Reading level: Grade 11
(FRE = 51   FI = 15   FK = 11)
Available from: library loan (out of print)

208

Morse, Bradford W. "Government obligations, aboriginal peoples and section 91(24) of the Constitution Act, 1867." In **Aboriginal peoples and government responsibility; Exploring federal and provincial roles**, edited by David C. Hawkes, 59-91. Ottawa: Carleton University Press, 1989.

In this historical review of federal and provincial interpretation of section 91(24) of the Constitution, Morse considers the impact of entrenchment of aboriginal rights under section 35(1). He raises questions about the extent of the trust responsibility found in the *Guerin* case. [Note: findings in the *Sparrow* case (1990) answer a number of the questions raised by Morse.]

Reading level: College
(FRE = 34   FI = 18   FK = 15)
Cost: $21.95

209

Robinson, Eric, and Henry Bird Quinney. **The infested blanket: Canada's Constitution-genocide of Indian nations.** Winnipeg: Queenston House, 1985. 168 p.

The "infested blanket" is a metaphor for the proposed constitutional changes and the possible effects on native peoples. It provides a critical appraisal of the Assembly of First Nation's approach to the constitutional conference. Written by/for First Nations.

Reading level: Grade 12
(FRE = 44   FI = 16   FK = 14
Cost: $9.95

210

Sanders, Douglas E. "The Constitution, the provinces, and aboriginal peoples." In **Governments in conflict? Provinces and Indian nations in Canada**, edited by J. Anthony Long and Menno Boldt, with Leroy Little Bear, 151-174. Toronto: University of Toronto Press, 1988.

Sanders examines section 91(24) of the Constitution Act, which assigns responsibility for Indian people to the federal government. He discusses how the courts interpret the section and the resulting conflicts that arise in federal and provincial jurisdiction.

Reading level: College
(FRE = 19   FI = 20   FK = 16)
Cost: $18.95

211

Sterritt, Neil J. "Aboriginal sovereignty and Canadian sovereignty: Bridging the gap." **Parliamentary Government** 10(2) (1991): 16-18.

Using the Gitksan-Wet'suwet'en case now before the courts, the author argues that political compromise is required to bring together First Nations and Canadian viewpoints on self-government and sovereignty. He suggests constitutional entrenchment of the inherent right to self-government.

Reading level: College
(FRE = 42   FI = 17   FK = 14)

Aboriginal title — British Columbia

212
Delgamuukw and the aboriginal land question: Conference Program, September 10 & 11, 1991, Victoria Conference Centre. Victoria, B.C.: University of Victoria, School of Public Administration, 1992.

Experts on aboriginal rights review the *Delgamuukw* case and reasons for judgment. Papers presented by anthropologists, historians, lawyers, and federal and provincial government representatives discuss their interpretation of the decision. Unedited conference audio tapes are also available.

Reading level: Grade 12
(FRE = 14   FI = 17   FK = 13)
Available from: Institute for Research on Public Policy
Cost: not available
Conference audio tape available from University of Victoria: $40

213
Time immemorial. Ottawa: National Film Board of Canada, 1991. Film or videocassette; 57 minutes; colour; sound.

This film documents the Nisga'a Nation's struggle for settlement of its land claims issue. It recounts culture clashes, lobbying efforts of the Nisga'a in Ottawa, Victoria, and England, the 1970s *Calder* case, and the first provincial government delegation to enter Nisga'a land to begin negotiations. These events are linked by beautiful footage of the spectacular Nass Valley.

Cost: 26.95
Rental: $5/week

214
British Columbia. Supreme Court. **Delgamuukw et al. v. the Queen: Reasons for judgment.** Victoria: Queen's Printer, March 8, 1991. 394 p.

This lengthy document presents Chief Justice Allan McEachern's reasons for judgment in the major land claims court case. The case involves the hereditary chiefs of the Gitksan and Wet'suwet'en, who sought legal claim to their aboriginal rights of ownership and jurisdiction over their homelands. The decision reflects an astonishing hold to the colonialist ideology of nineteenth-century British imperialism. The case is now in the court of appeals.

Reading level: College
(FRE = 31   FI = 20   FK = 16)
Cost: $29.95

215
British Columbia Claims Task Force. **The report of the British Columbia Claims Task Force, June 18, 1991.** Vancouver: The Task Force, 1991. 84 p.

In December 1990, this task force's 19 recommendations were accepted by the majority of First Nations, the province, and federal government. The recommendations are about the development of treaty negotiations to resolve the land issue, the formation of a B.C. Treaty Commission, funding of the negotiations, dispute resolution, development of interim measures, and public education and information programs on the negotiations.

Reading level: Grade 12
(FRE = 33   FI = 17   FK = 13)
Cost: free

216

Canada. Indian and Northern Affairs. **British Columbia Indian comprehensive claims.** Vancouver: Indian and Northern Affairs, January 1991. 1 map: scale = 1:2,000,000; colour.

This newly revised map of B.C. outlines the 22 comprehensive claims areas submitted by the Nisga'a; Kitwancool; Gitksan-Wet'suwet'en; Haisla; Tahltan; Nuu-chah-nulth; Haida; Heiltsuk; Nuxalk; Nazko Klukus; Kaska-Dene; Carrier-Sekani; Alkali Lake; Taku Tlingit; Kootenay; Tsimshian; Nlaka'pamux; Kwakiutl; Sechelt; Musqueam; and Homalco.

Cost: free

217

Canada. Indian and Northern Affairs. **Building a new relationship with First Nations in British Columbia: Canada's response to the report of the B.C. Claims Task Force.** Ottawa: Indian and Northern Affairs, 1991. 8 p.

The B.C. Claims Task Force report of July 1991 proposes political negotiation as a means of resolving comprehensive claims in the province. In this booklet, the federal government affirms acceptance of the report. Included are the federal government's positions on the proposed negotiating process and the scope of negotiations.

Reading level: College
(FRE = 24   FI = 22   FK = 17)
Cost: free

218

Cassidy, Frank, and Norman Dale. **After native claims? The implications of comprehensive claims settlements for natural resources in British Columbia.** Lantzville, B.C.: Oolichan Books; Halifax: Institute for Research on Public Policy, 1988. 230 p.

The B.C. business community has expressed some uncertainty and concern about the impact of land claims settlement on use and management of natural resources. Using data from technical and government reports, interviews with groups involved, and examination of other jurisdictions (NWT, Alaska, Quebec, Greenland), the authors identify three possibilities for resolving the problem. The three scenarios would involve fisheries, forestry, and non-renewable resource industry sectors and include (1) business-oriented "partners in development," (2) co-management either as allies or advocacies, (3) preservation-oriented "homeland and hinterland." Each scenario takes into account government, First Nations, and third-party concerns and interests. The authors suggest that some disruption can be expected as new roles are defined, but in the long term, conflicts will be reduced and enhancement of resources emphasized.

Reading level: Grade 12
(FRE = 40   FI = 16   FK = 12)
Cost: $12.95

219

Cassidy, Frank, ed. **Reaching just settlements: Land claims in British Columbia; Proceedings of a conference held February 21-22, 1990.** Lantzville, B.C.: Oolichan Books; Halifax: Institute for Research on Public Policy, 1991. 153 p.

The conference goal was to encourage constructive dialogue between groups affected by land claims. Highly readable papers present the viewpoints of participants, including First Nations representatives, labour, industry, environmental groups, and municipal government. Topics include historical and legal background; emerging trends; what the federal and provincial governments can do; and the next three years. Six appendices reprint documents related to land claims, including the Premier's Council on Native Affairs Progress Report and the First Nations Congress Response.

Reading level: Grade 12
(FRE = 50   FI = 16   FK = 12)
Cost: $14.95

220

Drake-Terry, Joanne. **The same as yesterday: The Lillooet chronicle the theft of their lands and resources.** Lillooet, B.C.: Lillooet Tribal Council, 1989. 341 p.; illus.; bibliography.

This history of the Lillooet from a First Nations' viewpoint begins with an overview of European exploration and settlement of the continent. The impact of colonial policy on the Lillooet people is documented with archival records and oral history. Accounts are given of the decimation of the people and their resources during the fur trade, the gold rush, and the settlement of the southern interior of the province. Resistance to reserve allotments leads the Lillooet chiefs to sign a declaration of ownership of traditional territories in 1911.

Reading level: College
(FRE = 38   FI = 20   FK = 17)
Cost: $29.95

221

Gisday, Wa, and Delgam Uukw. **The spirit in the land: The opening statement of the Gitksan and Wet'suwet'en hereditary chiefs in the Supreme Court of British Columbia, May 11, 1987.** Gabriola, B.C.: Reflections, 1989. 91 p.; photographs.

Two hereditary chiefs present a forthright and stirring account of the basis for court action by the Gitksan and Wet'suwet'en people in their claim to title and jurisdiction. The historical and current facts in these sketchy descriptions create reader interest in the pending arguments and the possible outcome of this critical event in Canada's legal history.

Reading level: College
(FRE = 40   FI = 18   FK = 14)
Available from: Office of the Hereditary Chiefs of the Gitksan and Wet'suwet'en People
Cost: $13.95

222

Glavin, Terry. **A death feast in Dimlahamid.** Vancouver: New Star Books, 1991. 200 p.

Glavin skilfully blends past and present to provide an inside view of the Gitksan and Wet'suwet'en people's struggle in the legal system. Although use of hereditary names complicates the story, the interweaving of leadership profiles with descriptions of the peoples' history, culture, beliefs, and folklore makes this an informative and thought-provoking book.

Reading level: Grade 12
(FRE = 46   FI = 16   FK = 13)
Cost: $14.95

Frog dish
Haida

photo: J. Gijssen

223

Mathias, Chief Joe, and Gary Yabsley. "Conspiracy of legislation." **B.C. Studies** 89 (Spring 1991): 34-45.

The authors examine critical Canadian legislation and conclude that the intent has been to eliminate Indian rights, if not the very presence of Indians and "Indianness," from society. References to court cases and acts take up more than half of this short, highly technical article.

Reading level: University
(FRE = 35   FI = 25   FK = 21)
Cost: $10

224

Monet, Don, and Skanu'u. **Colonialism on trial.** Gabriola Island, B.C.: New Society Publishers, 1992. 224 p.; illus.

Don Monet, an artist and activist, attended the Gitksan and Wet'suwet'en sovereignty court case over a three-year period. He presents portraits, sketches, court transcripts, newspaper reports, and photographs of the trial. These are interwoven with a sensitive portrayal of the Gitksan, the Wet'suwet'en, and their supporters' emotions and views of the case. Co-authored by Ardyth Wilson, Gitksan speaker.

Reading level: Grade 10
(FRE = 64   FI = 12   FK = 10)
Cost: $19.95 (paperback); $57.95 (hardbound)

225

Office of the Hereditary Chiefs of the Gitksan and Wet'suwet'en People. **On Indian land.** Hazelton, B.C.: Office of the Hereditary Chiefs of the Gitksan and Wet'suwet'en People, 1986. 1/2" VHS videocassette; 60 minutes; colour; sound.

The history and culture of the Gitksan/Wet'suwet'en people is presented in the context of today and what has led them to their current court case. Use this film in conjunction with "The Spirit in the Land" (#221).

Cost: $36

226

Protocol between the chiefs of the Secwepemc Nation, the chiefs of the Okanagan Nation, the chiefs of the Nlaka'pamux Nation and the chiefs of the Stl'atl'imx Nation. Merritt, B.C.: Nicola Valley Tribal Council [unpublished document], August 15, 1990. 12 p.

This document contains the re-affirmation and re-dedication of four First Nations of B.C. to the Spences Bridge protocol of July 1910 and 1911. The original declaration to Sir Wilfred Laurier, Prime Minister of Canada, states that these nations are the "rightful owners of our tribal territory, and everything pertaining thereto. We have always lived in our country; at no time have we ever deserted it, or left it to others." The document also contains the Declaration of the Tahltan Tribe, October 1910. *Recommended by Norma Hall, Nicola Valley Tribal Council.*

Reading level: University
(FRE = 18   FI = 28   FK = 24)
Available from: Nicola Valley Tribal Council
Cost: photocopying cost

227

Rauent, Daniel. **Without surrender, without consent: A history of Nishga land claims.** Vancouver: Douglas & McIntyre, 1984. 244 p.

This work examines the history of the Nishga people, the arrival of Europeans, the resultant losses, and the rise of nationalism among the Nishga people. It is well researched and authoritative. Rich with related readings or as a reference for instructors. Good introduction. Very readable.

Reading level: Grade 10
(FRE = 63   FI = 14   FK = 10)
Available from: library loan (out of print)

228

Sewid-Smith, Daisy. "In time immemorial." **B.C. Studies** 89 (Spring 1991): 16-32.

This intriguing history lesson demonstrates use of the International Phonetic Alphabet in an oral history which tells of the Nimpkish people's presence on the land prior to the great flood. Highly personalized accounts of contemporary events, including first contact and relations with governments, show that by 1990 there had been little progress in resolving B.C. land and resource issues.

Reading level: Grade 8
(FRE = 68   FI = 11   FK = 8)
Cost: $10

229

Sterritt, Neil J. "Unflinching resistance to an implacable invader." In **Drumbeat: Anger and renewal in Indian country**, edited by Boyce Richardson, 265-294. Toronto: Summerhill Press, 1989.

Sterritt describes the confrontations resulting from the Gitksan and Wet'suwet'en assertion of jurisdiction over resources in their traditional territories. He recounts government refusal to recognize tribal management plans for fisheries and describes fisheries officers' raids on fishing grounds and the blockades of logging roads that Gitksan and Wet'suwet'en peoples have used in their resistance to intrusions into their territories.

Reading level: Grade 12
(FRE = 50   FI = 16   FK = 12)
Cost: $14.95

230

Tennant, Paul. **Aboriginal peoples and politics: The Indian land question in British Columbia, 1849-1989.** Vancouver: University of British Columbia Press, 1990. 324 p.

This comprehensive book on land claims in British Columbia extends from the first Douglas treaties to the political negotiations, blockades, and court cases of the 1980s. It documents the development of modern political activity and of First Nations' organizations in this century. Recommended for its excellent overview of aboriginal rights and title and the post-contact political history of the B.C. Indian people.

Reading level: College
(FRE = 38   FI = 15   FK = 15)
Cost: $19.95

231

Tizya, Rosalee. **The Indian Nations story: A summary.** Vancouver: Union of B.C. Indian Chiefs, June 1986. 31 p.

Speaker/activist Rosalee Tizya thoroughly researched North American and Canadian First Nations' history and legislation to present this summary of post-contact history. Traditional philosophy is discussed in conjunction with self-government, impact of legislative acts, and court cases.

Reading level: College
(FRE = 39   FI = 19   FK = 15)
Cost: photocopying cost

Aboriginal title — Canada

232

Bartlett, Richard H. **Aboriginal water rights in Canada: A study of aboriginal title to water and Indian water rights.** Calgary: Canadian Institute of Resources Law, 1988. 235 p.

Bartlett presents the first in-depth study of this topic. He examines the scope and priority of water rights under aboriginal title and as part of appropriations for reserve lands. He discusses abrogation of water rights by government, flooding in violation of aboriginal rights, and contemporary agreements (James Bay and Inuvialuit Final Agreement). He suggests that a mechanism be established to promote joint First Nations-government management of the resource. Includes tables of statutes and cases cited.

Reading level: College
(FRE = 34   FI = 18   FK = 14)
Cost: $30

233

Canada. Indian and Northern Affairs. **Comprehensive land claim agreement in principle between Canada and the Dene Nation and the Métis Association of the Northwest Territories.** Ottawa: Indian and Northern Affairs Canada, 1988. 179 p.

This agreement in principle covers financial information; renewable resources; land and resources; administration of lands and resources; and relationships with other claimants. The appendices contain a description of implementation provisions and the land selection process.

Reading level: Not applicable (legislative document)
Cost: free

234

Canada. Indian and Northern Affairs. **Comprehensive land claims policy.** Ottawa: Indian and Northern Affairs Canada, 1987. 26 p.

This brief document outlines Canada's policy on comprehensive land claims negotiations. It clarifies the government's position and shows that extinguishment is central to their negotiating stance. The policy provides a strong incentive to begin debate on land claims.

Reading level: College
(FRE = 31   FI = 21   FK = 15)
Cost: free

235

Canada. Indian and Northern Affairs. **Comprehensive land claim agreement in principle between the government of Canada, the Council for Yukon Indians and government of the Yukon.** Ottawa: Indian and Northern Affairs Canada, 1989. 140 p.

The agreement in principle, dated May 29, 1989, states the terms, conditions, and processes to be used in an umbrella final agreement. Matters covered in this agreement include eligibility and enrolment processes; land issues including tenure and management of settlement lands; land quantum; definition of boundaries; conservation and use of renewable resources; financial compensation; resource royalty-sharing; self-government agreements; implementation processes; and dispute resolution. This is a highly technical report.

Reading level: Not applicable (legislative document)
Cost: free

236

Canada. Indian and Northern Affairs. **Information sheets on comprehensive claims.** Ottawa: Indian Affairs and Northern Development, 1992.

Each information sheet on comprehensive claims in British Columbia is approximately four pages in length and is published as new events in comprehensive claims occur. The information presents government's views.

Reading level: College
(FRE = 22   FI = 20   FK = 16)
Cost: free

237

Council of Yukon Indians. **Land claim agreements information booklet.** Whitehorse: Council for Yukon Indians.

Recommended by Sharon Jacobs, Council for Yukon Indians.

Reading level: Not available
Cost: free

238

Canada. Task Force to Review Comprehensive Claims Policy. **Living treaties: Lasting agreements: Report of the task force to review comprehensive claims policy.** Ottawa: Indian Affairs and Northern Development, 1985. 132 p.; bibliography

Submissions by First Nations and review of legal issues support the task force's recommendations to change the 1973 policy on comprehensive claims ("In All Fairness"). The report reviews such contentious issues as government requirement of extinguishment of rights; restrictions on eligibility criteria and on the number of groups that may enter the claims process; and the unwieldy negotiation process. A new comprehensive claims policy and process is proposed and discussed in depth.

Reading level: College
(FRE = 24   FI = 21   FK = 17)
Cost: free

239

Elliot, David W. "Aboriginal title." In **Aboriginal peoples and the law; Indian, Métis and Inuit rights in Canada**, edited by Bradford Morse, 48-121. Ottawa: Carleton University Press, 1989.

Although Canadian courts are beginning to accept First Nations' definitions of title, legal issues remain to be clarified. Elliot considers the following four basic questions in relation to Canadian and U.S. court decisions: (1) To what extent is aboriginal title recognized in the various sources of law? (2) What is the scope and content of these rights? (3) What can terminate or restrict aboriginal rights? (4) Is there a legal obligation on the part of the government to compensate for any termination or restriction?

Reading level: College
(FRE = 39   FI = 19   FK = 15)
Cost: $31.95

240

Hodgins, Bruce W., and Jamie Benidickson. **The Temagami experience: Recreation, resources, and aboriginal rights in the northern Ontario wilderness.** Toronto: University of Toronto Press, 1989. 370 p.

This history of the Temagami region of northern Ontario begins with the Ice Age and settlement by the Temagami people approximately 5,000 years ago. Traditional land use, the fur trade, exploration, establishment of the Temagami Forest Reserve, the area's use as a recreation area, and events that contribute to the alienation of land and resources from the Temagami First Nation are recounted. The Bear Island court case is reviewed and federal-provincial negotiations on the Temagami land claim are examined.

Reading level: Grade 12
(FRE = 47   FI = 16   FK = 13)
Cost: $19.95

241

Lubicon Lake Indian Band. **Lubicon Lake Indian Band Inquiry: Discussion paper.** Lubicon Lake, AB: Lubicon Lake Indian Band, 1988. 91 p.

This discussion paper presents the position of the Lubicon Band, the federal and provincial governments, and third-party interests on the many issues raised by the band, including land and resources; environmental protection programs; employment and training; general compensation for losses in land claims; oil and gas revenues; treaty benefits; loss of livelihood from trapping and hunting and future losses; and compensation for trespass, waste, and destruction of culture and life-style. Self-government and the right to determine membership are also discussed.

Reading level: University
(FRE = 28   FI = 23   FK = 19)
Available from: Microlog No. 88 - 04006
Cost: $20

242

Manitoba. Lands Branch. **Crown lands handbook on Indian land claims in Manitoba.** Winnipeg: Manitoba Natural Resources, Lands, 1988. 202 p.

This handbook summarizes the Manitoba government policy and the status of negotiations on claims of bands, including treaty land entitlement, land affected by hydro-electric dam flooding, and expropriation. A provincial summary is provided along with information (including maps) on specific band claims.

Reading level: College
(FRE = 33   FI = 19   FK = 14)
Available from: Microlog 88 - 05726
Cost: $30

243

Matchewan, Jean-Maurice. "Our long battle to create a sustainable future." In **Drumbeat: Anger and renewal in Indian country,** edited by Boyce Richardson, 137-166. Toronto: Summerhill Press, 1989.

In 1988 Barriere Lake Algonquins camped on Parliament Hill to protest logging and encroachments on their hunting and fishing territories: territories that are now La Verendrye Wildlife Reserve in Quebec. Government failure to address their claims led, a year later, to the Algonquins blockading logging roads in the reserve. Chief Matchewan describes his people's history from the time their territories were recognized by the 1763 Royal Proclamation up to the 1989 blockade, when they were charged with public nuisance and contempt of court. These blockades represent attempts to prevent further environmental damage to their unceded territories.

Reading level: Grade 11
(FRE = 54   FI = 15   FK = 11)
Cost: $14.95

244

Morse, Bradford W. **Providing land resources for aboriginal peoples.** Background Paper No. 16. Kingston: Institute of Intergovernmental Relations, Queen's University, 1987.

It is anticipated that land will be reaffirmed as aboriginal land as a result of settlement of land claims, treaty renegotiations, or other agreements. This publication examines legal issues involved, beginning with possible mechanisms for transfer of crown or non-crown land. A number of options are then identified for making the transfers. The kind of ownership or title (e.g., freehold, equitable estate, etc.) is examined in light of aboriginal people's concern that the land base be preserved and protected from future alienation.

Reading level: University
(FRE = 28   FI = 20   FK = 17)
Cost: $10

245

Moss, Wendy. **Aboriginal land claims issues.** Ottawa: Library of Parliament, Research Branch, 1990. 22 p.

This short paper provides a synopsis of specific claims and comprehensive claims policy. It discusses such issues as aboriginal title extinguishment ("superseded by law"), conflict of interest, and exclusion of self-government agreements from land claims agreements.

Reading level: College
(FRE = 36   FI = 18   FK = 14)
Available from: Canada Communications Group, Microlog 91 - 04886
Cost: $3.50

246

Moss, Wendy. "The implementation of the James Bay and Northern Quebec Agreement." In **Aboriginal peoples and the law; Indian, Métis and Inuit rights in Canada**, edited by Bradford Morse, 684-693. Ottawa: Carleton University Press, 1989.

The 1976 James Bay and Northern Quebec Agreement is considered the first modern treaty and is seen as indicator of government relations in future agreements. In this article, Moss presents a concise appraisal of its implementation. She gives an overview of events leading up to the agreement and a summary of its provisions, discusses the mechanisms established to implement the agreement, and reviews problems being encountered by the Cree and Inuit as a result of federal and provincial governments' failure to comply with the agreed terms.

Reading level: College
(FRE = 18   FI = 36   FK = 14)
Cost: $31.95

Totem
Alert Bay

photo: Alexis MacDonald-Seto

247

O'Reilly, James. "Indian land claims in Quebec and Alberta." In **Governments in conflict? Provinces and Indian nations in Canada,** edited by J. Anthony Long and Menno Boldt, with Leroy Little Bear, 139-147. Toronto: University of Toronto Press, 1988.

O'Reilly examines provincial involvement in land claims. Focusing on the Quebec government's actions during construction of the James Bay hydro dam, he maintains that provincial governments have little interest in settlement of aboriginal title. He argues that such a settlement conflicts with their desire to maintain total control over land, resources, and other areas of provincial jurisdiction. The Alberta government's position on the Lubicon claims is also briefly discussed.

Reading level: College
(FRE = 19   FI = 20   FK = 16)
Cost: $18.95

248

Potts, Gary. "Last-ditch defence of a priceless homeland." In **Drumbeat: Anger and renewal in Indian country,** edited by Boyce Richardson, 201-228. Toronto: Summerhill Press, 1989.

Potts chronicles the 112-year struggle of the Teme-augama Anishnabai against encroachment onto their traditional territories. Although unsurrendered, the land was declared a timber reserve by the Ontario government in 1901. Despite opposition from First Nations and environmental groups, extensive clear-cut logging was allowed in the area. Chief Potts describes his people's history and culture, and successive governments' failure to address their claims. He disputes the Bear Island ruling of the Ontario Court of Appeal disallowing Teme-augama Anishnabai claims on the basis that they were party to the Robinson-Huron Treaty of 1850. He uses federal archival records to support his argument.

Reading level: University
(FRE = 22   FI = 25   FK = 21)
Cost: $14.95

249

Richardson, Boyce. "Wrestling with the Canadian system: A decade of Lubicon frustration." In **Drumbeat: Anger and renewal in Indian country,** edited by Boyce Richardson, 229-264. Toronto: Summerhill Press, 1989.

Historically, treaties were signed to extinguish First Nations' land title, thus enabling development of an area. The federal government maintains the Lubicon were signatories to Treaty 8, signed in 1899. The Lubicon argue that their land remains unsurrendered, pointing out that the Department of Indian Affairs did not enter their area until 1939. Although the Lubicon have challenged intrusions in the courts, land development has proceeded, to the detriment of traditional life-styles. This article documenting their struggle includes the 1985 appeal to the International Human Rights Commission, the boycott of the Calgary Olympic Games in 1986, and subsequent government treatment of their claims.

Reading level: College
(FRE = 35   FI = 19   FK = 15)
Cost: $14.95

250

Sarazzin, Greg. "220 years of broken promises." In **Drumbeat: Anger and renewal in Indian country,** edited by Boyce Richardson, 167-200. Toronto: Summerhill Press, 1989.

The 1760 Articles of Capitulation and the 1763 Royal Proclamation recognize the right of the Ottawa Valley Algonquins to enjoy traditional territories unmolested. In the ensuing two centuries governments have continuously ignored Algonquin title to traditional land. Chief Sarazzin of Golden Lake describes past efforts to resist encroachment and the more recent effort to arrive at a land claims agreement that will recognize title while preserving intact what is now Algonquin Park.

Reading level: College
(FRE = 36   FI = 19   FK = 15)
Cost: $14.95

251

Scotnicki, Christine. **Recent treaties in land claims and self-government: The James Bay Agreement, the Cree-Naskapi Act, the Western Arctic (Inuvialuit) claim settlement and the Sechelt Indian Band Self-Government Act.** Victoria, B.C.: School of Public Administration, University of Victoria, 1987. 147 p.

This publication contains summaries, in layperson's terms, of what are otherwise relatively inaccessible legal documents. Highlights and summaries of each of the agreements are provided. Produced for First Nations peoples. *Recommended and annotated by V. Starr & Associates.*

Reading level: Grade 10 (provided by annotator)
Cost: $25

252

Sutton, Imre, ed. **Irredeemable America: The Indians' estate and land claims.** Albuquerque, NM: University of New Mexico Press, 1985. 421 p.

This is a comprehensive compilation of writings by Indian and non-Indian authors involved in U.S. land litigation. All the authors claim that the court processes do not succeed and that the Indian people involved leave with a "loss of esteem" for courts and lawyers and "embittered" by the adversarial structure of the litigation. Decisions lacked sensitivity and cash settlements were unsatisfactory, they say.

Reading level: University
Cost: $27.50

253

Yukon Department of Education. **Land claim unit module for use in Grade 10.** Whitehorse: Yukon Department of Education, 1992.

Recommended by Sharon Jacobs, Council for Yukon Indians.

Reading level: Grade 10 (provided by annotator)
Cost: TBA

Aboriginal rights

254

Allen, Graham W., and Robert C. Strother. **Aboriginal law: Materials prepared for a Continuing Legal Education seminar held in Vancouver, B.C. on April 28, 1990.** Vancouver: Continuing Legal Education Society of British Columbia, 1990.

This publication contains four papers prepared for an aboriginal law seminar. In "Fishing rights and the *Sparrow* case," Marvin Storrow discusses Fisheries Act regulations before and after the entrenchment of aboriginal rights in the Constitution and the implications of the *Sparrow* decision. In "Sechelt Land Claim," Graham Allen discusses problems with the federal land claims policy. A reprint of the 1989 Sechelt Band Council document outlines Sechelt's philosophy and position on settlement of their claim. Other papers discuss self-government under current legislation and taxation issues in economic development (individual exemptions and corporate liabilities).

Reading level: College
(FRE = 30   FI = 20   FK = 17)
Cost: $7

255

Angus, Murray. **And the last shall be first: Native policy in an era of cutbacks.** Toronto: NC Press Ltd., 1991. 87 p.

This thought-provoking book was a project of the Aboriginal Rights Coalition (Project North), an ecumenical coalition of national churches, church bodies, and regional groups working in solidarity with First Nations. Murray examines current government policies on native Indians and how government fiscal restraints affect policies. Discussion topics include self-government, the Constitution, specific and comprehensive claims, environmental issues, court cases, and the Oka conflict.

Reading level: College
(FRE = 28   FI = 20   FK = 17)
Cost: $9.95

256

Assembly of First Nations. **Towards linguistic justice for First Nations.** Ottawa: The Assembly of First Nations, 1990. 73 p.

Historic government policies aimed at eradicating aboriginal languages have endangered many languages. This report is part of the Assembly of First Nations' efforts to develop a national program to protect First Nations languages. Part 1 provides an overview of language planning and government recognition of official and aboriginal language rights in the Constitution, in legislation, and in policy. Part 2 presents findings of a survey of language use and resources in 151 First Nations. The report concludes with recommendations on a language revitalization strategy, including constitutional entrenchment of language and cultural rights.

Reading level: College
(FRE = 24   FI = 20   FK = 16)
Cost: $15

257

Elias, Peter Douglas. "Aboriginal rights and litigation: History and future of court decisions in Canada." **Polar Record** 25 [152] (January 1989): 1-8.

Litigation is expected to become more common since First Nations are disillusioned with government's commitment to negotiated settlements of aboriginal rights. The author argues, however, that litigation is not the ideal solution, since the courts are becoming increasingly more demanding about proof of claims. The Royal Proclamation of 1763 and historic decisions are discussed as well as more recent developments. Elias summarizes the legal tests and proof that previous claimants have been required to present, but does not discuss the validity of these tests. The large volume of data required from lawyers and social scientists and the "murky and poorly charted waters" of aboriginal rights in the legal system lead Elias to suggest that the solution lies in the political realm.

Reading level: College
(FRE = 19   FI = 22   FK = 17)
Available from: Cambridge University Press
Cost: See publisher

258

MacDonald, Jake. "Fur and against." **Western Living** (March 2, 1992).

MacDonald visits a trapper on Lake Manitoba and an elementary school classroom in Kenora, Ontario, where an anti-trapping film is viewed. He discusses the origins of animal rights and interviews Inuit and Dene leaders on the trapping issue. He notes that a 1980 Yale survey found that "support for the animal rights movement comes from the wealthy, the educated, the unmarried and the childless ... such activists ranked precisely 20th in their knowledge of general biology and also scored lowest of all 20 groups in their desire to spend time outdoors and encounter wildlife." He also says, "animal rights activists ... are trying to persuade the Cree, the Inuit and thousands of other land-based people to exchange traditional lives for values they assume to be superior — their own."

Reading level: Grade 11
(FRE = 52   FI = 14   FK = 11)
Cost: $2.50

259

Moss, Wendy. **Aboriginal rights.** Ottawa: Library of Parliament, Research Branch, Law and Government Division, 1990. 16 p.

Section 35(1) entrenchment of aboriginal rights in the Canadian Constitution has placed some urgency on legally defining aboriginal rights. This will occur through negotiation or through litigation. In this short publication, Moss reviews the history of aboriginal rights and discusses federal policy and findings of landmark court cases. She highlights the 1982 entrenchment of aboriginal rights and the differing interpretations given to Section 35(1). Of particular interest is the chronology of aboriginal claims policy.

Reading level: University
(FRE = 24   FI = 22   FK = 18)
Available from: Canada Communications Group
Cost: $3.50

260

Patterson II, E. Palmer. "Andrew Paull and the early history of British Columbia Indian organizations." In **One century later: Western Canadian reserve Indians since Treaty 7**, edited by Ian A. L. Getty and Donald B. Smith, 43-54. Vancouver: University of British Columbia Press, 1978.

Patterson analyzes the history of B.C. Indian organizations through the life of Andrew Paull, a Squamish man, who played a key role in all phases. As Paull's life and political activities are traced, land claims initiatives evolve from protest by small units (1880-1915) to protest by larger organizational units (e.g., 1940s Native Brotherhood).

Reading level: Grade 12
(FRE = 38   FI = 17   FK = 13)
Available from: library loan (out of print)

261

Pelts: Politics and the fur trade. Ottawa: National Film Board of Canada, 1989. Film or videocassette; 57 minutes; colour; sound.

This film presents the many and often conflicting ethical, environmental, cultural, and economic concerns of Indian trappers, animal rights activists, and the fur industry. The Indian people firmly believe their way of life is being threatened, and they resent the imposition of non-Indian values in their traditional lands. Animal rights activists believe animals should not be killed for their fur.

Cost: $26.95
Rental: $5/week

262

Schellenberger, Stan. **The fur issue: Cultural continuity, economic opportunity.** Report of the Standing Committee on Aboriginal Affairs and Northern Development. Ottawa: Queen's Printer, 1986.

One of the few available papers that presents this aspect of the continuing confrontation of two cultures: traditional native populations and the non-native animal rights movement. This movement represents popular western culture and its new-found ethics for a relationship with the animal world. The Standing Committee heard presentations on the importance to native people of land-based activities (hunting, trapping, and fishing), their economic viability, and whether these activities were "evil, immoral or harmful to the environment," as represented by some groups.

Reading level: College
(FRE = 31   FI = 19   FK = 16)
Available from: library loan (out of print)

263

Union of British Columbia Indian Chiefs. **Indian water rights in British Columbia: A handbook.** Vancouver: Union of B.C. Indian Chiefs, 1991. 31 p.

This booklet was prepared over six years for the Union of B.C. Indian Chiefs by the law firm Mandell and Pinder, Thalassa Research Associates, and Nancy Sandy, in-house counsel of the UBCIC. Thorough research of archival materials, case law, and legislation is evident in both sections. Part 1 outlines the history of Indian water rights from pre-Confederation to 1939. Part 2 outlines legal arguments available to First Nations.

Reading level: University
(FRE = 23   FI = 24   FK = 20)
Cost: $12.95

Part III

Future

Self-government

264

Balance to be kept. Hazelton, B.C.: Office of the Hereditary Chiefs of the Gitksan and Wet'suwet'en, 1987. VHS videocassette; 30 minutes; colour; sound.

This video presents the Gitksan-Wet'suwet'en perspective on self-government. *Recommended and annotated by Vicky Russell, Office of the Hereditary Chiefs of the Gitksan and Wet'suwet'en.*

Cost: $69.95

265

Abele, Frances, and Katherine A. Graham. "High politics is not enough: Policies and programs for aboriginal peoples in Alberta and Ontario." In **Aboriginal peoples and government responsibility: Exploring federal and provincial roles**, edited by David C. Hawkes, 141-171. Ottawa: Carleton University Press, 1989.

The authors look at provincial involvement in aboriginal self-government in the provinces of Alberta and Ontario. A review of local conditions is followed by examples on how progress has been made in policy development and program delivery. Programs referred to include social services programs such as child welfare and corrections.

Reading level: University
(FRE = 17   FI = 22   FK = 18)
Cost: $21.95

266

Bartlett, Richard H. **Subjugation, self-management and self-government of aboriginal lands and resources in Canada.** Kingston, ON: Institute of Intergovernmental Relations, 1986. 102 p.

In this survey of law relating to aboriginal self-government of land and resources, Bartlett says that self-government of land and resources currently does not exist in Canada. He bases his conclusions on a review of federal and provincial legislation and local government agreements, including the Cree-Naskapi Act; the Sechelt Indian Band Self-Government Act; and the Inuvialuit Final Agreement. He argues that recognition of self-government must extend beyond what is available under local agreements.

Reading level: Grade 12
(FRE = 44   FI = 18   FK = 13)
Cost: $10

267

Boldt, Menno, and J. Anthony Long, with Leroy Little Bear. **The quest for justice: Aboriginal peoples and aboriginal rights.** Toronto: University of Toronto Press, 1985. 406 p.

Entrenchment of aboriginal rights in the Constitution significantly altered First Nations-government relations by requiring provincial participation in future negotiations. This book, sequel to the 1984 publication *Pathways to Self-determination*, examines hurdles being encountered as consensus is sought on aboriginal rights and self-government. The first of five parts presents a native perspective of the issues. The following sections discuss constitutional, judicial, and policy processes from government and First Nations viewpoints. The collection provides a good basis for discussion and debate.

Reading level: College
(FRE = 24   FI = 17   FK = 16)
Cost: $19.95

268

Canada. Parliament. House of Commons. Special Committee on Indian Self-Government. **Indian self-government in Canada.** Ottawa: Queen's Printer, 1983. 203 p.

This ground-breaking report is based on evidence from First Nations as well as research reports commissioned by the committee. It reviews existing powers and structures of First Nations government; fiscal arrangements with the federal government; and crown responsibility (trust relationship) to First Nations. The committee recommended fundamental restructuring of relations with First Nations, including constitutional entrenchment of self-government; dismantling of the department of Indians Affairs; and enactment of a First Nations Relations Act.

Reading level: Grade 12
(FRE = 37   FI = 17   FK = 13)
Available from: Microlog 84 - 00275
Cost: $30

269

Canada. Special Parliamentary Committee on Indian Self-Government. "Proposals for Self-Government." In **Arduous journey: Canadian Indians and Decolonization,** edited by Rick Ponting, 327-341. Toronto: McClelland and Stewart, 1986.

This is an abridgement of the 1983 report on self-government, in which the committee recommended restructuring First Nations-government relations. The article summarizes findings and major recommendations of the committee, which include entrenching self-government in the Constitution; replacing the Department of Indian Affairs with a Ministry of State for First Nations; and providing adequate land and resources to First Nations.

Reading level: Grade 12
(FRE = 37   FI = 17   FK = 13)
Cost: $19.95

270

Canadian Arctic Resources Committee. **Aboriginal self-government and constitutional reform: Setbacks, opportunities, and Arctic experiences.** Ottawa: Canadian Arctic Resources Committee, 1988. 168 p.

This book contains the speeches and discussion from a 1987 conference on self-government. Some presentations provide useful information on the topic, while others are largely rhetorical. Of greater interest is the panel discussion on Nunavut, the proposed Inuit government for the eastern Arctic. Major issues include when the government would be created and what its final form would be.

Reading level: Grade 12
(FRE = 48   FI = 16   FK=13)
Cost: $21.95

271

Cassidy, Frank, ed. **Aboriginal self-determination: Proceedings of a conference held September 30 - October 3, 1990.** Lantzville, B.C.: Oolichan Books; Halifax: Institute for Research on Public Policy, 1991. 284 p.

Presentations of conference participants, including First Nations, government, industry, and professionals, are reported under the four themes: "What is self-government?"; "How will it work?"; "Implementation"; and "The road to self-determination." The papers are diverse, thought-provoking, and at times provocative. Though a basic understanding of the issues is required, background papers in the appendices should be helpful. These papers examine self-government in the legal system and in government policy. The Assembly of First Nations' paper "Critique of the federal government's land claims policy" is excellent.

Reading level: Grade 12
(FRE = 48   FI = 16   FK = 12)
Cost: $14.95

272

Cassidy, Frank, and Robert L. Bish. **Indian government: Its meaning in practice.** Lantzville, B.C.: Oolichan Books, 1989. 186 p.

This book examines how First Nations have achieved a degree of self-government under existing federal and provincial legislation. The historical and legal basis of aboriginal self-government is reviewed and the differing viewpoints of First Nations and government highlighted. Self-government in 17 First Nations is demonstrated: how policy is developed, how programs and services are managed and delivered, and financing. Future directions are considered, and legislated self-government, such as in the Sechelt and the Cree-Naskapi acts, is discussed and constitutional entrenchment reconsidered.

Reading level: Grade 12
(FRE = 34   FI = 17   FK = 13)
Cost: $13.95

273

Collins, Theo. **The Sechelt Act and what it means.** Vancouver: Union of B.C. Indian Chiefs, 1988. 35 p.

This booklet was prepared for the UBCIC by Theo Collins, a native law student at the University of B.C. The controversial Sechelt Indian Band Self-Government Act is interpreted section by section for laypeople.

Reading level: Not applicable (legislative document)
Cost: $10.95

274

Franks, C. E. S. **Public administration questions relating to aboriginal self-government.** Kingston, ON: Institute of Intergovernmental Relations, Queen's University, 1987. 109 p.

Franks discusses traditional forms of First Nations government and the impact of non-aboriginal government on these institutions. He examines possible functions or responsibilities in self-government: who will participate in the government and the process of decision making. Specific administration questions relate to financing and policy making in First Nations governments, personnel development, and administration. Franks considers the role of intergovernmental relations and suggests that change to federal administration is crucial to successful implementation of self-government.

Reading level: University
(FRE = 17   FI = 23   FK = 18)
Cost: $10

Sign
Alert Bay

photo: Alexis MacDonald-Seto

275

Hawkes, David Craig. **Aboriginal self-government: What does it mean?** Kingston, ON: Institute of Intergovernmental Relations, Queen's University, 1985. 99 p.

Under section 37 of the Constitution Act, 1982, a series of First Ministers conferences were planned to address aboriginal issues. Discussions focus on self-government. The Institute did research on aboriginal self-government to support these conferences. In this technical background paper, different models of self-government are examined, using national and international examples. The opportunities and constraints of the models are discussed.

Reading level: College
(FRE = 22   FI = 19   FK = 14)
Cost: $12

276

Hawkes, David Craig. **Implementing aboriginal self-government: Problems and prospects.** Kingston, ON: Institute of Intergovernmental Relations, Queen's University, 1986. 83 p.

Hawkes reports on a workshop organized by the Institute of Intergovernmental Relations as part of the Institute's project on aboriginal people and constitutional reform. Participants include First Nations, federal, provincial, and territorial governments, and experts in the field. They examine self-government agreements as well as negotiating and financing issues. The plenary sessions and workshops are summarized. Workshop topics include education, resource management, and economic development. Appendices contain technical papers prepared for the conference.

Reading level: College
(FRE = 31   FI = 18   FK = 14)
Cost: $7

277

Hawkes, David Craig, and Allan M. Maslove. "Fiscal arrangements for aboriginal self-government." In **Aboriginal peoples and government responsibility: Exploring federal and provincial roles,** edited by David C. Hawkes, 93-137. Ottawa: Carleton University Press, 1989.

The authors discuss federal and provincial responsibility for financing self-government and propose a policy framework for funding aboriginal government, taking into account the degree of autonomy of the institution and level of economic, political, and administrative capacity. Examples used demonstrate that existing self-government agreements (summarized in an appendix) currently do not link political and fiscal autonomy.

Reading level: College
(FRE = 24   FI = 19   FK = 15)
Cost: $21.95

278

International Conference Towards Native Self-Reliance Renewal and Development (1984: Vancouver, B.C.). **Native self-reliance through resource development.** Vancouver: William F. Sinclair, 1985. 258 p.; illus.

This is a report of an international conference exploring native self-reliance through economic development. Papers presented include those by First Nations and government representatives and specialists from Canada, the United States, and overseas. Forestry, agriculture, non-renewable resources, and tourism are some of the topics covered. What works in economic development and the role of land claims in resource development are discussed. Questions to presenters are included in each section. Papers presented provide a good overview of the legislative, government policy, environmental, financial, and human resource aspects that affect native economic development.

Reading level: Grade 11
(FRE = 50   FI = 15   FK = 11)
Available from: library loan (out of print)

279

Long, Anthony, J., and Menno Boldt, eds. **Governments in conflict? Provinces and Indian nations in Canada.** Toronto: University of Toronto Press, 1988. 296 p.

During the past two decades, the provinces have assumed a greater role in aboriginal affairs. This collection of 17 papers by First Nations, government officials, and specialists in the field examine the resulting jurisdictional conflicts. The publication includes sections on roles and responsibilities of the three parties in constitutional negotiations; policy and program initiatives by the Ontario, B.C., and Quebec governments; and the provinces' involvement in land claims. Three papers discuss and compare aboriginal policies of Australia, the United States, and the Northwest Territories. The disparate viewpoints illustrate the challenges that lie ahead for self-government.

Reading level: College
(FRE = 19   FI = 20   FK = 16)
Cost: $18.95

280

Malone, Marc. **Financing aboriginal self-government in Canada.** Kingston, ON: Institute of Intergovernmental Relations, Queen's University, 1986. 64 p.

This paper addresses the critical issue of financing aboriginal self-government. Existing arrangements for financing aboriginal, municipal, regional, and provincial government are considered. Financing of aboriginal government is analyzed using four criteria: effectiveness, efficiency, equity, and autonomy. Six financing options are then proposed and assessed. These options range from maintaining the status quo to land claims settlement and regional government financing. The report concludes that constitutional entrenchment of self-government is necessary.

Reading level: University
(FRE = 12   FI = 23   FK = 19)
Cost: $7

281

Morse, Bradford, W. **Aboriginal self-government in Australia and Canada.** Kingston, ON: Institute of Intergovernmental Relations, Queen's University, 1984. 130 p.

This background work supports current dialogue on self-government in Canada. Description of the status on aboriginal people in Australia is comprehensive and provides a useful comparison with the experience of natives in Canada. Morse identifies and discusses similarities and differences and makes recommendations for further analysis.

Reading level: University
(FRE = 20   FI = 21   FK = 18)
Cost: $12

282

Penner, Keith. "Their own place: The case for a distinct order of Indian First Nation government in Canada." In **Governments in conflict? Provinces and Indian nations in Canada,** edited by J. Anthony Long and Menno Boldt with Leroy Little Bear, 31-37. Toronto: University of Toronto Press, 1988.

Penner, chair of the 1983 parliamentary committee to examine Indian self-government, discusses the committee report and the recommendations on recognizing First Nations' inherent right to self-government. He maintains that the federal government has a responsibility to begin a "reasonable exchange" with First Nations on recognizing and implementing self-government.

Reading level: College
(FRE = 34   FI = 19   FK = 15)
Cost: $18.95

283

Peters, Evelyn J. "Federal and provincial responsibilities for the Cree, Naskapi and Inuit under the James Bay and Northern Quebec, and Northeastern Quebec agreements." In **Aboriginal peoples and government responsibility: Exploring federal and provincial roles,** edited by David C. Hawkes, 173-242. Ottawa: Carleton University Press, 1989.

Peters provides a detailed review of federal and provincial responsibilities under the James Bay and Northern Quebec Agreement and the Northeastern Quebec Agreement. She describes and evaluates implementation in local and regional government, harvesting and the environment, economic development, education, and local services (specific clauses, along with supporting legislation, are identified in the appendices). Noting the problems encountered, Peters finds that there is need for not only a formal implementation mechanism but also political will on the part of the federal and provincial governments.

Reading level: University
(FRE = 20   FI = 22   FK = 19)
Cost: $21.95

284

Pointing, J. Rick. "Public opinion on aboriginal peoples' issues in Canada." **Canadian Social Trends** (Winter 1988): 9-17.

This 1986 public opinion poll shows that although there is widespread support for the general notion of increased self-determination, Canadians are wary of arrangements that involve special privileges for aboriginal people. Support is present, despite the fact that levels of knowledge and awareness of aboriginal issues were found to be generally low. Tables, bar graphs, and charts summarize the many issues explored in this study.

Reading level: College
(FRE = 28   FI = 20   FK = 16)
Cost: See publisher

285

Pratt, Alan. "Federalism in the era of aboriginal self-government." In **Aboriginal peoples and government responsibility: Exploring federal and provincial roles,** edited by David C. Hawkes, 19-57. Ottawa: Carleton University Press, 1989.

Pratt analyzes federal and provincial responsibility for programs and services for aboriginal people. He discusses federal responsibility under section 91(24) of the Constitution Act, 1867, and section 35 of the Constitution Act, 1982. He also considers provincial responsibility for delivery of services to all citizens under section 93 of the 1867 act. A review of case law relating to collective rights and equality includes discussion of the Guerin case, in which the courts found the crown has a fiduciary responsibility to Indian people. Unfortunately, he only provides a superficial treatment of Indian taxation under section 87 of the Indian Act.

Reading level: College
(FRE = 23   FI = 21   FK = 17)
Cost: $21.95

286

Taylor, John P., and Gary Paget. "Federal/provincial responsibility and the Sechelt." In **Aboriginal peoples and government responsibility: Exploring federal and provincial roles,** edited by David C. Hawkes, 297-348. Ottawa: Carleton University Press, 1989.

These authors discuss the federal and provincial roles and responsibilities under the Sechelt Band Self-Government Act. They present conditions among native people in B.C. and the Sechelt specifically and then highlight the objectives of the participants in the Sechelt Act. They describe the framework of the act and the legislative, financial, and administrative roles and responsibilities of the various governments. They discuss the implications of the act for the Sechelt, other First Nations, and the federal and provincial governments.

Reading level: College
(FRE = 24   FI = 20   FK = 17)
Cost: $21.95

287

Weinstein, John. **Aboriginal self-determination off a land base.** Kingston, ON: Institute of Intergovernmental Relations, Queen's University, 1986. 54 p.

Past discussion on self-government has centred on First Nations occupying traditional lands. This paper, by a former adviser to the Native Council of Canada and the Métis National Council, argues that consideration must be given to those living off a land base. A number of options are proposed that will enable all aboriginal people to participate in self-governing institutions. Examples cited illustrate community and regional consultations involving urban-based people in planning self-government.

Reading level: College
(FRE = 17   FI = 22   FK = 17)
Cost: $7

288

Wright, D. **Indian self-government.** Ottawa: Library of Parliament, Research Branch, 1987. 13 p.

Wright discusses Indian self-government historically and considers changes in federal policy since 1950. The 1983 report of the Special Committee on Indian Self-Government is reviewed, and an overview of related parliamentary action is provided, including the Sechelt Band Self-Government Act. The author also discusses alternative funding arrangements and includes a chronology of events concerning Indian self-government since 1763.

Reading level: College
(FRE = 28   FI = 20   FK = 15)
Cost: $20

Appendices & Indexes

Appendix 1
Publishers and distributors

Alliance of Tribal Nations
510 - 68 Water Street
Vancouver, BC
V6B 1A4

Arsenal Pulp Press
100 - 1062 Homer Street
Vancouver, BC
V6B 2W9

Assembly of First Nations
5th Floor - 55 Murray Street
Ottawa, ON
K1N 5M3

B.C. Provincial Curriculum Publications
Marketing Department, Open Learning Agency
P.O. Box 94000
Richmond, BC
V6Y 2A2

British Columbia Provincial Museum – *see*
Royal British Columbia Museum

British Columbia Reports
B.C. Report News Magazine Ltd.
103 - 1161 Melville Street
Vancouver, BC
V6E 2X7

B.C. Royal Commission on Health Care and Costs
(Orders: Crown Publications)

B.C. Studies
University of British Columbia
218 - 2029 West Mall
Vancouver, BC
V6T 1Z2

B.C. Teachers' Federation
2235 Burrard Street
Vancouver, BC
V6V 3H9

Black Rose Books
3981 boul. St.-Laurent, 4th Floor
Montreal, PQ
H2W 1Y5
(Orders: University of Toronto Press)

Cambridge University Press
40 West 20th Street
New York, NY 10011-4211

Canada Communications Group Publishing
Room B1001
45 boul. Sacre-Coeur
Hull, PQ
K1A 0S9
(819) 956-4802

Note: Canadian government publications may also be purchased through government publications agents including Duthie Techncial and Professional Books, the UBC bookstore, and World Wide Books and Maps in Vancouver.

Canadian Arctic Resources Committee
412 - 1 Nicholas Street
Ottawa, ON
K1N 7B7

Canadian Bar Association
902 - 50 O'Conner Street
Ottawa, ON
K1P 6L2

Canadian Environmental Assessment Research Council
13th Floor, Fontaine Building
200 boul. Sacre-Coeur
Hull, PQ
K1A 0H3

Canadian Nature Federation
453 Sussex Drive
Ottawa, ON
K1N 6Z4

Appendix 1

Canadian Institute of Resources Law
430 Biological Sciences Building
University of Calgary
Calgary, AB
T2N 1N4

Canadian Journal of Family Law
Faculty of Law, U.B.C.
Room 165, 1822 East Mall
Vancouver, BC
V6T 1Y1

Canadian Museum of Civilization
700 Block Asticou Centre
Hull, PQ.
K1A OM8
(Orders: University of Toronto Press)

Canadian Review of Sociology and Anthropology
Canadian Sociology and Anthropology Association
Concordia University
1455 Boul. de Maisonneuve W.
Montreal, PQ
H3G 1M8

Canadian Review of Sociology and Anthropology
Available in Microform from:
University Michrofilms International
300 North Zeeb Road
Ann Arbor, MI 48106
or
30-32 Mortimer Street
London W1N 7RA, England

Canadian Social Trends
Statistics Canada
Communications Division
3rd Floor, RH Coats Building
Ottawa, ON
K1H 0T6

Canadian Speeches – *see* **Canada Communications Group Publishing**

Carlton University Press
B443, Loeb Building
Colonel By Drive
Ottawa, ON
K1S 5B6

Carswell
2075 Kennedy Road
Scarborough, ON
M1T 3V4

College of New Caledonia Press
3330 - 22nd Avenue
Prince George, BC
V2N 1P8

Continuing Legal Education Society of B.C.
1148 Hornby Street
Vancouver, BC
V6Z 2C3

The Council of the Haida Nation
P.O. Box 589
Massett, Haida Gwaii, BC
V0T 1MO

Council for Yukon Indians
22 Nisutlin Drive
Whitehorse, YK
Y1A 2S5

Crown Publications
546 Yates Street
Victoria, BC
V8W 1K8
Telephone: (604) 386-4636

Department of Indian Affairs and Northern Development
Public Information Kiosk
Communications Branch
Ottawa, ON
K1A 0H4

Detselig Enterprises
465 - 301 14th Street, N.W.
Calgary, AB
T2N 2A1

Douglas & McIntyre, Ltd.
1615 Venables Street
Vancouver, BC
V5L 2H1

Appendix 1

Fifth House
1 - 128 2nd Avenue N.
Saskatoon, SK
S7K 2B2
(Orders: University of Toronto Press)

First Nations Resource Council
10036 Jasper Ave.
Edmonton, AB
T5J 2W2

FM Studio for the Children's Project
P.O. Box 86926
North Vancouver, BC
V7L 4P6

Gray's Publishing Ltd.
P.O. Box 5487, Station B
Victoria, BC
V8R 6S4

Heritage House Publishing
5543 129th Street
Surrey, BC
V3W 4H4

Highway Book Shop
R.R. 1
Cobalt, ON
P0J 1C0

Hurtig Publishers – *see* McClelland and Stewart

Indian and Northern Affairs – *see* Department of Indian Affairs and Northern Development

Institute of Intergovernmental Relations
Queen's University
Kingston, ON
K7L 3N6

Institute for Research on Public Policy
P.O. Box 3670
South Halifax, NS
B3J 3K6

J. Lorimer & Company
35 Britain Street
Toronto, ON
M5A 1R7
(Orders: University of Toronto Press)

Journal of Child Care
(new name **Journal of Child and Youth Care**)
University of Calgary Press
816 MacKimmie Library Tower
404 University Court
2500 University Drive NW
Calgary, AB
T2N 1N4

Law Reform Commission of Canada
1130 Albert Street, 7th Floor
Ottawa, ON
K1A 0L6

Legal Perspectives – *see* Schools Programs, Legal Services Society of B.C.

Legal Resource Centre
Legal Services Society of B.C.
Suite 300, Box 3
1140 West Pender Street
Vancouver, BC
V6E 4G1

Lillooet Tribal Council
P.O. Box 1420
Lillooet, BC
V0K 1V0

Little, Brown and Company Canada
148 Yorkville Avenue
Toronto, ON
M5R 1C2

McClelland and Stewart
900 - 481 University Avenue
Toronto, ON
M5G 2E9

McGill - Queen's University Press
3420 McTavish Street
Montreal, PQ
H3A 1X9

Macmillan of Canada
29 Birch Avenue
Toronto, ON
M4V 1E2

Appendix 1

Manitoba Justice Inquiry
(Orders: Canada Communications Group Publishing)

Marvin Melnyk Assoc. Ltd.
P.O. Box 220
Queenston, ON
L0S 1L0

Microlog
Micromedia Limited
165 Hotel de Ville
Hull, PQ
J8X 3X2
Telephone: (819) 770-9928
From area codes 204, 306, 403, 604, 709, please dial 1-800-567-1914. All others, 1-800-567-9669.
Fax: (819) 770-9265

Price Structure

No. of Pages	Microlog Price
1 - 100	$20.00
101 - 200	$30.00
201 - 400	$45.00
401 - 600	$55.00
601+	$0.12/page

Microfiche copies: $10/title

Ministry of Native Affairs (B.C.)
(new name: Ministry of Aboriginal Affairs)
5th Floor, 712 Yates Street
Victoria, BC
V8V 1X4

Moricetown Indian Band
R.R. 1, Site 15, Box 1
Smithers, BC
V0J 2N0

Monthly Review Press
122 W. 27th Street, 10th Floor
New York, NY 10001

National Film Board of Canada
100 - 1045 Howe Street
Vancouver, BC
V6Z 2B1
Telephone: (604) 666-0716
Fax: (604) 666-1569

National Museum of Canada – *see* **Canadian Museum of Civilization**

Native Adult Education Resource Centre
Okanagan College
Box 610
Salmon Arm, BC
V1E 4N7

Native Law Centre
University of Saskatchewan
141 Diefenbaker Centre
Saskatoon, SK
S7N 0W0

Native Programs
Legal Services Society
Suite 300, Box 3
1140 West Pender Street
Vancouver, BC
V6E 4G1

Native Studies Review
Native Studies Department
104 McLean Hall
University of Saskatchewan
Saskatoon, SK
S7N 0W0

Nature Canada
Canadian Nature Federation
453 Sussex Drive
Ottawa, ON
K1N 6Z4

NC Press
401 - 260 Richmond Street W.
Toronto, ON
M5V 1W5
(Orders: University of Toronto Press)

New Society Publishers
Box 189
Gabriola Island, BC
V0R 1X0

New Star Books Ltd.
2504 York Avenue
Vancouver, BC
V6K 1E3

Nicola Valley Tribal Council
Box 188
Merritt, BC
V0K 2B0

Appendix 1

Nlaka'pamux Nation Tribal Council
Box 430
Lytton, BC
V0K 1Z0

Northern Justice Society
c/o Continuing Education
Simon Fraser University
Burnaby, BC
V5G 1S6

Office of the Hereditary Chiefs of the Gitksan and Wet'suwet'en People
P.O. Box 229
Hazelton, BC
V0J 1Y0

Office of the Hereditary Chiefs
Vancouver Branch
200 - 73 Water Street
Vancouver, BC
V6N 1A1

Ontario Institute for Studies in Education
252 Bloor Street W.
Toronto, ON
M5S 1V6

Oolichan Books
P.O. Box 10
Lantzville, BC
V0R 2H0

Parliamentary Government
275 Slater Street, 5th Floor
Ottawa, ON
K1P 5H9

Pemmican Publications
412 McGregor Street
Winnipeg, MB
R2W 4X5

Perception: A Canadian Journal of Social Comment
Canadian Council on Social Development
55 Parkdale Avenue
P.O. Box 3505, Station C
Ottawa, ON
K1Y 4G1

Pica Press
(Orders: University of Alberta Press)

Plains Publishing
15879 116th Avenue
Edmonton, AB
T5M 3W1

Polar Record
Scott Polar Research Institute
Cambridge University Press
Edinburgh Building
Shaftesbury Road
Cambridge, CB22RU, England

Prairie Justice Research
Room 515, Library Building
University of Regina
Regina, SK
S4S 0A2

Prentice-Hall Canada, Inc.
1870 Birchmount Road
Scarborough, ON
M1P 2J7

Prince George Native Friendship Centre
144 George Street
Prince George, BC
V2L 1P9

Provincial Museum of Natural History and Anthropology – *see* **Royal British Columbia Museum**

Queen's Printer (B.C.)
(Orders: Crown Publications)

Queen's Printer (Manitoba)
Legislative Buildings
177 Lombard Avenue
Winnipeg, MB
R3B 0W5

Queenston House Publishing Co. Ltd.
102 Queenston Street
Winnipeg, MB
R3N 0W5

Appendix 1

Reflections Publishing
P.O. Box 178
Gabriola Island, BC
V0R 1X0

Royal British Columbia Museum
Parliament Buildings
Victoria, BC
V8V 1X4

Royal Commission on Health Care Costs
(Orders: Crown Publications)

Royal Commission on Aboriginal Peoples
(Orders: Canada Communications Group Publishing)

Royal Commission on the Donald Marshall, Jr. Prosecution
(Orders: Canada Communications Group Publishing)

Schools Program
Legal Services Society
Suite 300, Box 3
1140 West Pender Street
Vancouver, BC
V6E 4G1

Sechelt Indian Band
P.O. Box 740
Sechelt, BC
V0N 3A0

Secwepemc Cultural Education Society
345 Yellowhead Highway
Kamloops, BC
V2H 1H1

Smithsonian Institution
7100 - 470 L'Enfant Plaza
Washington, D.C. 20560

Social Planning and Research Council of B.C.
106 - 2182 West 12th Avenue
Vancouver, BC
V6K 2N4
Telephone: (604) 736-8118

Solicitor General of Canada
(Orders: Canada Communications Group Publishing)

Sono Nis Press
1745 Blanshard Street
Victoria, BC
V8W 2J8

Supply and Services Canada
Canadian Government Publishing Centre
Ottawa, ON
K1A 0S9

Summerhill Press
52 Shaftesbury Avenue
Toronto, ON
M4T 1A2
(Orders: University of Toronto Press)

Talonbooks
201 - 1019 East Cordova Street
Vancouver, BC
V6A 1M8
(Orders: University of Toronto Press)

Theytus Books
P.O. Box 218
Penticton, BC
V2A 6K3

Tillacum Library – *see* **Marvin Melnyk Assoc. Ltd.**

U'Mista Cultural Centre
Front Street
Alert Bay, BC
V0N 1A0

Union of B.C. Indian Chiefs
Chief's Mask Bookstore
73 Water Street
Vancouver, BC
V6B 1A1

University of Alberta Press
141 Athabasca Hall
University of Alberta
Edmonton, AB
T6G 2E8

University of British Columbia Press
6344 Memorial Road
Vancouver, BC
V6T 1W5

Appendix 1

University of California Press
2120 Berkeley Way
Berkeley, CA 94720

University of Guelph
Guelph, ON
N1G 2W1

University of Manitoba Press
244 - 106 Curry Place
University of Manitoba
Winnipeg, MB
R3T 2N2

University of New Mexico Press
1720 Lomas Boulevard, N.E.
Albuquerque, NM 87131-1591

University of Ottawa Press
603 Cumberland Street
Ottawa, ON
M5S 1A6

University of Toronto Press
5201 Dufferin Street
Downsview, ON
M3H 5T8

University of Victoria
Centre for Public Sector Studies
School of Public Administration
P.O. Box 1700
Victoria, BC
V8W 2Y2

University of Windsor
Windsor, ON
N9B 3P4

Vancouver Public Library
750 Burrard Street
Vancouver, BC
V6Z 1X5

Viking Penguin Inc.
2801 John Street
Markham, ON
L3R 1B4

Watson & Dwyer
232 Academy Road
Winnipeg, MB
R3M OE7

Western Living
300 S.E. Tower
555 West 12th Avenue
Vancouver, BC
V5Z 4L4

Wilfred Laurier University Press
Wilfred Laurier University
Alumni Hall
Waterloo, ON
N2L 3C5

Women's Press
233 - 517 College Street
Toronto, ON
M6G 4A2
(Orders: University of Toronto Press)

Yukon Department of Education
Curriculum Development
Government of Yukon
Box 2703
Whitehorse, YK
Y1A 2C6

Appendix 2
Speakers

Ktunaxa/Kinbasket Tribal Council
S.S. 3, Site 15, Comp. 14
Mission Road
Cranbrook, BC
V1C 4H4
Telephone: (604) 489-2464
Fax: (604) 489-5760

Sophie Pierre	Land claims
	History
Wilfred Jacobs	Land claims
	Fisheries
Wayne Choquette	Archaeological history
	Fisheries
	Natural resources
Leo Williams	History
	Culture
Marian Michel	History
	Culture

Native Adult Education Resource Centre
Box 610
Salmon Arm, BC
V1E 4N7
Telephone: (604) 832-3221
Fax: (604) 832-2771

Art Napolean	Community development
	Life skills
	Self-government
Don Sawyer	Native curriculum development
	Accommodating native students
	Native adult education

Office of the Hereditary Chiefs of the Gitksan and Wet'suwet'en
P.O. Box 229
Hazelton, BC
V0J 1Y0
Telephone: (604) 842-6511
Fax: (604) 842-6828

Herb George	Land claims
	Self-government
	Native law and resource management
Ardythe Wilson	Self-government
Ralph Michel	Fisheries — aboriginal rights
Marvin George	Forestry — aboriginal rights

Prince George Native Friendship Centre
144 George Street
Prince George, BC
V2L 1P9
Telephone: (604) 563-3568
Fax: (604) 563-0924

Dan George	PGNFC policies/history
	Land claims
	Native leadership skills
Barry Seymour	PGNFC policies/history
	Land claims
	Native business/management
Thone Chow	Native people/history
	Alcohol/drug programs
	Native healing/spirituality

Appendix 2

Barb Burrows WOW program
Streetworkers'
   program/project
Reconnect

Jane Inyallie Native healing/spirituality
Alcohol/drug abuse
Native healing circles

United Native Nations
300 - 33 East Broadway
Vancouver, BC
V5T 1VI
Telephone: (604) 879-2420
Fax: (604) 879-3778

Ron George Native title
Land claims

Ernie Crey Community services
Child welfare

Nelson Mayer Social issues of urban
   aboriginal peoples

Rosalee Tizya Self-government

Subject index

Listed by entry number

Aboriginal rights, 3, 11, 18, 56, 80, 87, 89, 94, 100, 116, 119, 161, 168, 200, 208, 210, 212, 213, 214, 224, 232, 233, 235, 254 - 2 63, 266, 267, 284

Aboriginal title, 5, 7, 8, 11, 12, 18, 50, 55, 56, 57, 58, 85, 89, 90, 125, 142, 168, 211, 212, 213, 214, 215, 216, 217, 218, 220, 2 21, 222, 224, 226 - 231, 233, 234, 235, 239, 240, 247, 248, 249, 250, 251, 252, 253, 266, 267

Adoption, 135, 139, 148, 164

Agreements (land settlements), 193, 197, 219, 232, 233, 234, 235, 237, 244, 246, 251, 266, 283

Alcohol/drugs, 130

Algonquin, 186, 207, 243, 250

Art, 40, 41, 42, 53

Assimilation, 21, 60, 73, 74, 75, 78, 80 - 84, 108, 111, 134, 137, 138, 153, 155, 223

Band councils, 15, 19, 40, 96, 99, 100, 105

Beaver, 27, 29, 31

Bella Coola, 25

Bibliographies, 178

Biographies, 10

Carrier, 30, 31, 78, 83, 84

Chilcotin, 83, 84

Child welfare, 128, 134, 135, 137 - 150, 158, 265

Claims, comprehensive, 216, 217, 233, 234, 235, 236, 238, 240, 240, 241, 242, 244, 245, 248, 249, 255, 259, 271

Claims, specific, 115, 117, 123, 245, 255

Coast Salish, 25, 32, 33, 34, 35, 51

Constitution, 60, 87, 92, 94, 100, 119, 200 - 211, 255, 256, 259, 267, 268, 272, 280, 285

Cree, 67, 159

Cree-Naskapi, 251, 266, 272, 283

Criminal justice system, 114, 128, 144, 150, 164 - 185, 265

Culture — B.C., 1, 5, 9, 11, 25, 28

Culture — Canada, 9, 11, 13, 24

Curriculum materials, 10, 16, 17, 253

Debtor/creditor, 104

Dene, 233

Department of Indian Affairs, 4, 58, 107, 121, 268, 269

Directories, 1, 2, 180

Discrimination, 144, 155, 176, 182, 183, 185

Early travellers, 59

Economic development, 108, 125

Education, 4, 16, 17, 40, 92, 97, 128, 151 - 164, 278

Employment, 156

Environment, 34, 186 - 199, 255, 278, 283

Estates, 96, 99, 100

Family law, 19

Films and videos, 14, 26, 71, 108, 186, 187, 189, 198, 213, 225, 264

Fishing rights, 100, 114, 229, 254

Fur trade, 6, 9, 47, 50, 54, 64 - 72, 86, 220, 240

Genocide, 59

Gitksan, 21, 25, 36, 76, 169, 211, 212, 214, 221, 222, 224, 225, 229

Gold Rush, 76

Government relations, 3, 5, 6, 8, 58, 66, 73, 78, 85, 90, 91, 92, 100, 108, 112 - 123, 125, 128, 129, 133, 154, 155, 200, 210, 211, 214, 220, 228, 229, 246, 274, 279

Haida, 25, 38, 39, 191

Haisla, 25

Health, 4, 97, 100, 124, 126, 127, 128, 129, 133

Heiltsuk, 25

Subject index

History — B.C., 1, 6, 7, 9, 21, 28, 31, 65, 66, 230, 260
History — Canada, 9, 54, 62, 64, 120, 231
Homalco, 51
Housing, 97
Hunting rights, 100
Hydro-electric developments, 189, 194, 199, 232, 242

Indian Act, 5, 8, 15, 19, 20, 47, 58, 93 - 112, 115, 119, 231
International laws, 55, 56, 57, 61, 63, 116
Inuit, 119, 193, 197, 232, 251, 266
Innu, 187, 188

James Bay, 67, 154, 189, 194, 232, 246, 251, 283
Jay Treaty, 90, 100

Kamloops Indian Band, 95
Klahoose, 51
Kwakiutl, 21, 25, 26, 40, 41, 42, 43, 107, 129, 131, 133, 228

Labour, 15, 102
Land use and management, 19, 85, 96, 99, 103, 105, 242, 244, 269
Language, 1, 23, 34, 35, 42, 46, 49, 256
Law, 15, 19, 89, 100, 212, 214, 223
Lillooet, 198, 220
Literacy, 157, 163
Local government, 47, 121
Logging (clear cut), 186, 191, 229, 243, 248
Lubicon, 241, 247, 249

Marshall, Donald, Jr., 165, 170
Membership, 94, 96, 97, 98, 99, 100, 108
Metis, 5, 8, 54, 64, 72, 118, 119, 134, 171, 233, 287
Mi'kmaq, 89, 114, 165, 170
Mining, 191
Missionaries, 6, 31, 45, 47, 51, 55, 57, 61, 62, 63, 66, 73 - 84

Mohawk, 90, 113, 117, 123, 131
Mount Currie, 154
Museums, 20, 40

Natural resources, 32, 40, 186, 218, 241, 243, 266, 278
Nisga'a, 25, 31, 76, 79, 154, 213, 227
Nlaka'pamux, 48, 195, 196, 198, 226
Non-status Indians, 119
Northwest Rebellion, 54, 60
Nuu-chah-nulth, 25, 43, 44, 45, 46, 75
Nuxalk, 43

Oil and gas, 193
Oka, 60, 113, 117, 120, 123, 255
Okanagan, 47, 48, 226
Ontario, 73, 78
Oowekeeno, 25

Policing, 172, 180
Potlatch, 12, 21, 26, 40, 41, 44, 45, 107, 222
Public opinion, 152, 284
Pulp mills, 191

Quebec, 207, 246, 247

Racism, 182, 185
Recreation, 40
Religion, traditional, 11, 22, 34, 40, 231
Reserves — B.C., 7, 45, 47, 50, 51, 220
Reserves — Canada, 60, 85, 100
Reserve lands, 95, 96
Residential school, 30, 31, 78, 108, 138, 153, 155, 158, 159, 160
Royal Proclamation of 1763, 11, 58, 100, 111, 119, 243, 250, 257

Secwepemc, 226
Sekani, 31
Sechelt, 49, 100, 251, 254, 266, 272, 273, 286, 288

Subject index

Self-government, 3, 5, 8, 90, 94, 110, 114, 128, 151, 161, 162, 164, 168, 174, 202, 203, 204, 211, 231, 241, 254, 255, 256, 264 - 288

Shuswap, 50, 83

Sliammon, 51

Socio-economic conditions, 4, 8, 11, 12, 30, 47, 52, 67, 69, 70, 86, 125, 129, 131, 139, 156, 176, 177

Spallumcheen Indian Band, 138, 141, 142, 143, 147

Stalo, 159, 198

Statistics, 4, 7, 54, 97, 127, 135, 139, 145, 176, 284

Stein River, 195, 196

Stl'atl'imx, 226

Students, 130

Taxation, 15, 19, 93, 95, 105, 109, 254, 285

Tahltan, 226

Temagami, 240, 248

Tlingit, 25, 53

Trapping rights, 258, 261, 262

Treaty 8, 31, 88, 91, 249

Treaties, 5, 8, 11, 58, 60, 85 - 92, 94, 100, 111, 115, 119, 161, 168, 199, 200, 215, 242, 250

Treaties, Vancouver Island, 87, 88, 230

Tsimshian, 25, 52, 76, 80, 81

Twin tracking, 198

Urbanization, 8, 132, 146

Uranium mining, 190, 192

Water rights, 232, 263

Wet'suwet'en, 36, 37, 77, 211, 212, 214, 221, 224, 225, 229

White Paper, 1969, 111, 112, 128

Women, 30, 38, 64, 72, 97, 98, 100, 108, 116

Yukon, 235, 237

Title index

Listed by entry number

220 years of broken promises, *250*

A

Aboriginal land claims issues, *245*

Aboriginal law: Materials prepared for a Continuing Legal Education seminar held in Vancouver, B.C. on April 28, 1990, *254*

Aboriginal peoples and politics: The Indian land question in British Columbia, 1849-1989, *230*

Aboriginal peoples and constitutional reform: What have we learned?, *206*

Aboriginal peoples of British Columbia, The: A profile, *1*

Aboriginal peoples, self-government, and constitutional reform, *203*

Aboriginal rights, *259*

Aboriginal rights and government wrongs: Uranium mining and neo-colonialism in northern Saskatchewan, *192*

Aboriginal rights and litigation: History and future of court decisions in Canada, *257*

Aboriginal rights in international law: Human rights, *116*

Aboriginal self-determination off a land base, *287*

Aboriginal self-determination: Proceedings of a conference held September 30 - October 3, 1990, *271*

Aboriginal self-government: What does it mean?, *275*

Aboriginal self-government and constitutional reform: Setbacks, opportunities, and Arctic experiences, *270*

Aboriginal self-government in Australia and Canada, *281*

Aboriginal self-government in education in Canada, *162*

Aboriginal sovereignty and Canadian sovereignty: Bridging the gap, *211*

Aboriginal title, *239*

Aboriginal water rights in Canada: A study of aboriginal title to water and Indian water rights, *232*

Adoption and the Indian child, *135*

Adoption of native Canadian children, The, *148*

After native claims? The implications of comprehensive claims settlements for natural resources in British Columbia, *218*

Alexandrine Bulls of 1493, The: Pseudo-Asiatic Documents, *63*

Analysis of native Indian admissions to the B.C. correctional system for 1975, *176*

And the last shall be first: Native policy in an era of cutbacks, *255*

Andrew Paull and the early history of British Columbia Indian organizations, *260*

Annotated 1990 Indian Act, The: Including related treaties, statutes and regulations, *100*

As long as the rivers run: Hydro-electric development and native communities in western Canada, *199*

Aspects of aboriginal rights in international law, *56*

Assimilation tools: then and now, *101*

Assu of Cape Mudge: Recollections of a coastal Indian chief, *40*

B

Balance to be kept, *264*

Basic departmental data — 1990, *4*

Between Ports Alberni and Renfrew: Notes on West Coast peoples, *46*

Blockade: Algonquins defend the forest, *186*

Box of treasures, *42*

British Columbia Indian comprehensive claims, *216*

British Columbia Indian treaties in historical perspective, *88*

Building a new relationship with First Nations in British Columbia: Canada's response to the report of the B.C. Claims Task Force, *217*

C

Caesars of the wilderness: Company of adventurers, *68*

Canadian Encyclopedia, The, *11*

Canadian Indian, The, *5*

Canadian native children: Have child welfare laws broken the circle? *137*

Cariboo mission, The: A history of the Oblates, *83*

Chiefly feasts: The enduring Kwakiutl potlatch, *41*

Chiefs of the sea and sky: Haida heritage sites of the Queen Charlotte Islands, *39*

Child welfare and the Native Indian peoples of Canada, *142*

Child welfare programme of the Spallumcheen Indian Band in British Columbia, The, *141*

Child welfare services for urban Native Indians, *146*

Children of tomorrow's great potlatch, The, *158*

Chronicles of pride: A journey of discovery, *10*

Chilliwacks and their neighbors, The, *35*

Coast Salish essays, *34*

Colonialism on trial, *224*

Columbus: His enterprise, *59*

Comprehensive land claim agreement in principle between Canada and the Dene Nation and the Métis Association of the Northwest Territories, *233*

Comprehensive land claim agreement in principle between the government of Canada, the Council for Yukon Indians and government of the Yukon, *235*

Comprehensive land claims policy, *234*

Conspiracy of legislation, *223*

Constitution, the provinces, and aboriginal peoples, The, *210*

Title index

Contact and conflict: Indian-European relations in British Columbia, 1774-1890, *66*

Covenant chain, The, *89*

Creating little dominions within the Dominion: Early Catholic schools in Saskatchewan and British Columbia, *159*

Crown lands handbook on Indian land claims in Manitoba, *242*

D

Dancing around the table, *200*

David confronts Goliath: The Innu of Ungaga versus the NATO Alliance, *188*

Death feast in Dimlahamid, A, *222*

Debtor-creditor law on reserve, *104*

Delgamuukw and the aboriginal land question: Conference Program, September 10 & 11, 1991, Victoria Conference Centre, *212*

Delgamuukw et al v. the Queen: Proceedings at trial, *36*

Delgamuukw et al v. the Queen: Reasons for judgment, *214*

Developing sustainability: A native/environmentalist prescription for third-level government, *195*

Devil and Mr. Duncan, The, *80*

Discovery of America and reform thought at the papal court in the early Cinquecento, The, *61*

During my time: Florence Edenshaw Davidson, a Haida woman, *38*

E

Effective instruction of native adults: 1-6, *16*

Environmental assessment and aboriginal claims: Implementation of the Inuvialuit Final Agreement, *197*

Error in judgement, An: The politics of medical care in an Indian/white community, *133*

Examination of the evolving concept of band councils, their authorities and responsibilities, and their statutory instruments of power, An, *105*

F

Federal and provincial responsibilities for the Cree, Naskapi and Inuit under the James Bay and Northern Quebec, and Northeastern Quebec agreements, *283*

Federal and provincial responsibility in the Métis settlements of Alberta, *118*

Federal perspectives on Indian-provincial relations, *121*

Federal/provincial responsibility and the Sechelt, *286*

Federalism in the era of aboriginal self-government, *285*

Final report: Task force on aboriginal peoples in federal corrections, *167*

Financing aboriginal self-government in Canada, *280*

First Canadians, The: A profile of Canada's native people today, *128*

Fiscal arrangements for aboriginal self-government, *277*

Title index

Flooding Job's garden, *189*

Foster care and adoption in Canada, *139*

Fundamental principles of Indian law, The, *15*

Fur and against, *258*

Fur issue, The: Cultural continuity, economic opportunity, *262*

G

Geese have lost their way, The, *194*

Give us good measure: An economic analysis of relations between the Indians and the Hudson's Bay Company before 1763, *70*

Governments in conflict? Provinces and Indian nations in Canada, *279*

Government obligations, aboriginal peoples and section 91(24) of the Constitution Act, 1867, *208*

Guide to native organizations and services in British Columbia, A, *2*

H

Handbook of North American Indians: Northwest Coast, Vol. 7, *25*

Health status of Canadian Indians and Inuit: Update 1987, *127*

High politics is not enough: Policies and programs for aboriginal peoples in Alberta and Ontario, *265*

Historical atlas of Canada: Vol. 1: From the beginning to 1800, *9*

Hunters and bombers, *187*

I

Impact of the white man, The: The history of Indians of British Columbia, *6*

Impacts of the 1985 amendments to the Indian Act (Bill C-31): Summary report, *97*

Implementation of the James Bay and Northern Quebec Agreement, The, *246*

Implementing aboriginal self-government: problems and prospects, *276*

In time immemorial, *228*

Incident at Restigouche, *114*

Indian Act and what it means, The, *106*

Indian Act of Canada, The, *94*

Indian band membership: An information booklet concerning new Indian band membership laws and the preparation of Indian band membership codes, *98*

Indian child and family services in Canada: Final report, *136*

Indian control of the Maritime fur trade and the Northwest Coast, *65*

Indian controlled child welfare: Adult survivors of child welfare stimulate their community to action, *138*

Indian country inside another Canada, *131*

Indian education in Canada. Vol. 2, The challenge, *154*

Indian government: Its meaning in practice, *272*

Indian land claims in Quebec and Alberta, *247*

Indian land holdings on reserve, *103*

Title index

Indian Nations story, The: A summary, *231*

Indian reserves and aboriginal lands in Canada; A homeland; A study in law and history, *85*

Indian self-government, *288*

Indian self-government & the Indian Act, *110*

Indian self-government in Canada, *268*

Indian water rights in British Columbia: A handbook, *263*

Indians and taxation in Canada, *93*

Infested blanket, The: Canada's Constitution-genocide of Indian nations, *209*

Information sheets on comprehensive claims, *236*

Inuvialuit Final Agreement, The, *193*

Iron hand upon the people, An: The law against the potlatch on the Northwest Coast, *21*

Irredeemable America: The Indians' estate and land claims, *252*

J

Judgement at Stoney Creek, *184*

Justice denied, *165*

K

Kahnewake, *113*

Katzie ethnographic notes, *33*

Knots in a string: An introduction to native studies in Canada, *3*

L

Labour law on reserve, *102*

Land claim agreements information booklet, *237*

Land claim unit module for use in Grade 10, *253*

Land, revenues and trusts review: Phase I report, *96*

Land, revenues and trusts review: Phase II report, *99*

Last-ditch defence of a priceless homeland, *248*

Law and order for Canada's indigenous people, *177*

Law of nations and the new world, The, *57*

Layperson's guide to treaty rights in Canada, A, *87*

Legacy Indian treaty relationships, *92*

Living treaties: Lasting agreements: Report of the task force to review comprehensive claims policy, *238*

Locking up natives in Canada: A report of the committee of the Canadian Bar Association on imprisonment and release, *179*

Lubicon Lake Indian Band: Inquiry: Discussion paper, *241*

M

MacPherson report on tradition and education: Towards a vision of our future, *161*

Making Canadian Indian policy: The hidden agenda 1968-1970, *112*

Many tender ties: Women in fur-trade society in western Canada, 1670-1870, *72*

Title index

Maps and dreams: Indians and the British Columbia frontier, *27*

Medicine man to missionary: Missionaries as agents of change among the Indians of southern Ontario, 1784-1867, *73*

Mi'kmaq and criminal justice in Nova Scotia, The: Research study prepared for the Royal Commission on the Donald Marshall, Jr., pros ecution, *170*

Mission on the Nass: The evangelization of the Nishga (1860-1990), *79*

Mission to Nootka, 1874-1900: Reminiscences of the west coast of Vancouver Island, *75*

Moon of wintertime: Missionaries and the Indians of Canada in encounter since 1534, *74*

Multicultural week, February 19-25, 1989: Aboriginal cultural diversity; A resource package for secondary schools, *12*

N

National Indian health transfer conference, The, *124*

Native children and the child welfare system, *140*

Native children in treatment: Clinical, social and cultural issues, *147*

Native children: white law, *144*

Native criminal justice research and programs: An inventory, *180*

Native English curriculum guidelines: A handbook for adult education, *17*

Native families in jeopardy: The child welfare system in Canada, *145*

Native health, *126*

Native justice consultations: Progress report and action plan, *166*

Native law, *19*

Native land claims in Canada: A study guide, *18*

Native lands then and now, *7*

Native liberty, crown sovereignty: The existing aboriginal right of self-government in Canada, *204*

Native literacy research report, *163*

Native North Americans: Crime, conflict and criminal justice: A research bibliography, *178*

Native people's access to justice, *164*

Native peoples and cultures of Canada: An anthropological overview, *24*

Handbook of North American Indians: Northwest Coast, Vol. 7, *25*

Native peoples in Canada: Contemporary conflicts, *8*

Native peoples: The Canadian experience, *13*

Native policing in Canada: A review of current issues, *172*

Native self-reliance through resource development, *278*

Native spirituality, past, present, and future, *22*

Native students with problems of addiction, *130*

Native studies of North Eastern B.C., *28*

Native victims in Canada: Issues in providing effective assistance, *169*

Title index

Natives and newcomers: Canada's heroic age reconsidered, 62

Not being a part of the way things work: Tribal culture and systemic exclusion in the Donald Marshall Inquiry, 183

Now you are my brother: Missionaries in British Columbia, 82

Nu-tka: The history and survival of Nootkan culture, 44

O

On Indian land, 225

One century later: Western Canadian reserve Indians since Treaty 7, 86

Other side of the ledger, The: An Indian view of the Hudson's Bay Company, 71

Our home and native land: A film and resource guide for aboriginal Canadians, 14

Our long battle to create a sustainable future, 243

Outstanding business: A native claims policy: Specific claims, 115

P

Papal division of the world and its consequences, The, 55

Pathways to success: Aboriginal employment and training strategy, 156

Pelts: Politics and the fur trade, 261

People of the Pines: The warriors and the legacy of Oka, 123

Periodic shortages, native welfare, and the Hudson's Bay Company 1670-1930, 69

PGNFC Newsletter, 132

Policy development for museums: A First Nations perspective, 20

Political and legal inequities among aboriginal peoples in Canada, The, 119

Potlatch: A strict law bids us dance, 26

Preventing and responding to northern crime, 175

Prison of grass: Canada from a native point of view, 54

Problems with the legislative base for native child welfare services, 150

Program review and evaluation assessment — criminal courtworkers, A: Native counselling services of Alberta, 173

Progress report and interim recommendations, 125

Proposals for self-government, 269

Proposed amendments to the Indian Act concerning conditionally surrendered land and band taxation powers, 95

Pros and cons of doing business on a reserve, 109

Prosecution or persecution, 107

Protection, civilization, assimilation: An outline history of Canada's Indian policy, 111

Protocol between the chiefs of the Secwepemc Nation, the chiefs of the Okanagan Nation, the chiefs of the Nlaka'pamux Nation and the chiefs of the Stl'atl'imx Nation, 226

Proud past: A history of the Wet'suwet'en of Moricetown, B.C., 37

Providing land resources for aboriginal peoples, *244*

Public administration questions relating to aboriginal self-government, *274*

Public opinion on aboriginal peoples' issues in Canada, *284*

Q

Queen's people, The: A study of hegemony, coercion, and accommodation among the Okanagan of Canada, *47*

Queesto: Pacheenaht chief by birthright, *45*

Quest for justice, The: Aboriginal peoples and aboriginal rights, *267*

R

Reaching just settlements: Land claims in British Columbia; Proceedings of a conference held February 21-22, 1990, *219*

Recent treaties in land claims and self-government: The James Bay Agreement, Cree-Naskapi Act, the Western Arctic (Inuvialuit) claim settlement and the Sechelt Indian Band Self-Government Act, *251*

Report on aboriginal peoples and criminal justice: Equality, respect and the search for justice, *181*

Report of the Aboriginal Justice Inquiry of Manitoba/Public inquiry into the administration of justice and aboriginal people, *182*

Report of the British Columbia Claims Task Force, June 18, 1991, *215*

Report of the Canadian Bar Association Committee on Aboriginal Rights in Canada: An agenda for action, *168*

Report to the Minister, Indian health and health care: Alert Bay, B.C., *129*

Resistance and renewal: Surviving the Indian residential school, *160*

Respective roles and responsibilities of federal and provincial governments, regarding the aboriginal peoples of Canada, *122*

Richard Cardinal: Cry from a diary of a Metis child, *134*

Right of aboriginal self-government and the Constitution, The: A commentary of the Royal Commission on Aboriginal Peoples, *202*

River is our home, The, *198*

Royal Commission on the Donald Marshall, Jr., Prosecution. Commissioners' report: Findings and recommendations, *185*

S

SA TS'E: Historical perspectives on northern British Columbia, *31*

Salish people, The: The local contribution of Charles Hill-Tout. Vol. 1: The Thompson and the Okanagan, *48*

Same as yesterday, The: The Lillooet chronicle the theft of their lands and resources, *220*

Sechelt Act and what it means, The, *273*

Selected documents from the Assembly of Manitoba Chiefs on the Meech Lake Accord, *201*

Title index

Separate and unequal: Indian and white girls at All Hallows School, 1884-1920, *155*

Shuswap history: The first 100 years of contact, *50*

Skyscrapers hide the heavens: A history of Indian-white relations in Canada, *60*

Sliammon life, Sliammon lands, *51*

Somewhere between, *108*

Spallumcheen Indian Band by-law and its potential impact on native Indian child welfare policy in British Columbia, The, *143*

Spirit in the land, The: The opening statement of the Gitksan and Wet'suwet'en Hereditary Chiefs in the Supreme Court of British Columbia, May 11, 1987, *221*

Spirit of the Alberta Indian treaties, The, *91*
Stein: The way of the river, *196*

Stoney Creek woman: The story of Mary John, *30*

Story of the Sechelt nation, The, *49*

Strangers in blood: Fur trade company families in Indian country, *64*

Struggle for recognition, The: Canadian justice and the Métis Nation, *171*

Study of education in context, A, *152*

Subarctic fur trade, The: Native social and economic adaptations, *67*

Subjugation, self-management and self-government of aboriginal lands and resources in Canada, *266*

Summer of 1990: Fifth report of the standing committee on aboriginal affairs, *117*

T

Taking of Indian lands in Canada, The: Consent or coercion?, *58*

Temagami experience, The: Recreation, resources, and aboriginal rights in the northern Ontario wilderness, *240*

Their own place: The case for a distinct order of Indian First Nation government in Canada, *282*

They call me father: Memoirs of Father Nicolas Coccola, *84*

Time immemorial, *213*

Tlingit Indians, The, *53*

Toward First Nations control of child welfare: A review of emerging developments in B.C., *149*

Towards linguistic justice for First Nations, *256*

Tradition and education: Towards a vision of our future, *151*

Trail to heaven: Knowledge and narrative in a northern native community, *29*

Tsimshian, The: Images of the past, views for the present, *52*

U

Unbroken assertion of sovereignty, An, *90*

Understanding native activism, *120*

Unflinching resistance to an implacable invader, *229*

Unlocking aboriginal justice: Alternative dispute resolution for the Gitksan and Wet'suwet'en people, *174*

Title index

Upper Stalo Indians of the Fraser Valley, British Columbia, The, *32*

V

Value of First Nations languages, The, *23*

Victorian missionary and Canadian Indian policy, A: Cultural synthesis vs cultural replacement, *78*

W

Warriors of the North Pacific: Missionary accounts of the Northwest Coast, the Skeena and Stikine Rivers, and the Klondike, 1829-1900, *76*

What are we? Chopped liver? Aboriginal affairs in the constitutional politics of Canada in the 1980s, *205*

Will Quebec recognize distinct native society?, *207*

Will to power: The missionary career of Father Morice, *77*

William Duncan of Metlakatla: A victorian missionary in British Columbia, *81*

Wisdom of the elders: Native traditions on the Northwest Coast: The Nuu-chah-nulth, Southern Kwakiutl and Nuxalk, *43*

Without surrender, without consent: A history or Nishga land claims, *227*

Wollaston: People resisting genocide, *190*

Wrestling with the Canadian system: A decade of Lubicon frustration, *249*

Y

Yakoun: River of life, *191*

You took my talk: Aboriginal literacy and empowerment, *157*